I Chose Life
and God Changed Mine

by Lauren Urrea

Copyright © 2019 by Lauren Urrea.

Requests for information should go to: lfurrea8@gmail.com

Cover design by Fistbump Media, LLC

All rights reserved. No part of this publication may be reproduced, stored in a retrieval system, or transmitted in any form or by any means—electronic, mechanical, photocopy, recording, or any other—without prior written permission of Lauren Urrea.

For information about special discounts for bulk purchases, please contact Lauren Urrea at lfurrea8@gmail.com.

ISBN-13: 9781793947512

Acknowledgments

"May He give you the desire of your heart and make all your plans succeed." – Psalm 20:4

A list of the people who have contributed to this journey would probably be enough to fill a whole separate book. Without each of you, this story may have been quite different. You may never truly understand the inexpressible gratitude I have for the part you played in helping me find the desires of my heart and succeed at the plans that were known to God long before this story began.

First and foremost, I am infinitely thankful for the grace and faithfulness the Lord has shown me through this experience. He deserves any and all glory that this book may bring.

None of this would have been possible without my incredible husband, Mateo Urrea. Literally none of it (but you will read about that soon enough). I know I've said it before, but I'll say it a million more times: Thank you for staying. Thank you for instantly fulfilling your responsibility as a father, for being the first voice of reason and encouragement, and for loving and encouraging me through the hardest time in our life. I am grateful for your heart every single day, and love you more than you will ever know.

To my parents, MarLane and Ron Knuppel, there is not a "thank you" that will ever be enough. You have lived out 1 Peter 4:8 to the fullest, and I am forever grateful for the million and one ways you have encouraged and supported me in this process. From day one, you showed me what deep, unconditional love looks like; a lesson I know will be valuable with my own children. You have been my biggest "cheerleaders," regardless of the challenges I've faced. You have sacrificed endlessly to help me achieve my goals and bring life to my dreams. I think I speak for Adrianna as well when I say that I have been beyond blessed by you both and I would have never made it this far without you. I love you both so, so very much.

To my brother, Matthew Knuppel, thank you for being everything I could have ever hoped for in a "big" brother. Two years younger, but infinitely more intuitive, you have been my greatest confidant and source of biblical wisdom. You have always known how to make me laugh, which many times throughout this process has been all that I really needed. Your love for the Lord and His Word has been such an inspiration to me, and I am certain will continue to be an inspiration to many others. She may not fully understand it yet, but Adrianna is so very lucky to have you for an uncle.

To my in-laws, Juan, Claudia, and Simon Urrea, thank you for your love and support of me, Mateo, and the kids. You raised your son to be such an honorable man, husband, and father. You have been his living example of perseverance, dedication, and hard work. I am so grateful to you for all you have done to help support us through the good and bad. Thank you, most importantly, for the love you continually show to our children.

To Susie Amos, my "Gabriel" and the volunteers at the Blue Ridge Women's Center, thank you for being the light in my darkest hour, and for being the first to show me that "nothing would be impossible with Him" (Luke 1:37). I know I am not the only one you have encouraged to choose life. You may never know how great an impact you have had on this world in that way, but know this: your impact on me was life-changing. I am ever grateful for you.

To my St. John and Community of Faith family, thank you for being the hands and feet of Jesus. One of my fears was the shame I would face at church, and I am grateful to say I never did. Many of you were quick to walk beside me, pray for me, hug me, encourage me, and pour love into Adrianna's life and my own. You all frequently showed a Christlike love to me and my family, and I was blessed to have you in my life when I needed it most.

To my best friend, Claire McKinney, thank you for thinking of me that very first day, and for every day forward when you walked through the valley with me. Your positive outlook and encouragement were instantaneous and you continued to be one of my biggest supporters through it all. I will forever be grateful for your presence when I needed it more than anything, for praying with me at 7-Eleven, and for holding my hand during my darkest hour. You are the perfect living example of what it means to be a best friend.

To the many other family members and friends, there are far too many of you to list and thank to the degree that you deserve. You know who you are. Please know each and every one of you are adored by me, and with deepest gratitude I say THANK YOU for the prayers, words of encouragement, hugs, advice, baby items, and love. It took a village to get to this point, and you all make up a very large part of it!

To Kate Motaung and Fistbump Media, thank you for all of your hard work on this book. Thank you also for being so patient and helpful as you guided me through the editing and formatting process. You were such a blessing and pleasure to work with!

Finally, to my first child, Adrianna. Thank you for being you. You are only a little over seven years old right now, but your life is the reason for all the words that follow. This book has been a dream of mine for years, with the initial intent being that you alone would one day have it to read. My hope is that as you read it, your faith would be strengthened in knowing that God has had amazing plans for you all along. God knew what I didn't from the very beginning, that I would need you more than I could have ever imagined and that your life would change mine for the better, forever. I am the lucky one, my dear. Though unexpected, you were and always will be one of my life's greatest blessings. I love you to the moon and back.

After graduating from high school, I may have told you that my plans for the future included graduation from college, medical missions, medical school, marrying the man of my dreams, and starting a family. But on November 29th, 2010, God revealed His very different plan—a plan that included the unexpected miracle of life that grew inside me. Unplanned by me, but known and designed by the Creator of the Universe.

The beginning of my story starts here.

Table of Contents

Hope for Gabriel 1
Its Heart is Already Beating 3
Driving for Three 6
Healing in the Holy Land 8
Peanut Wants Waffles 11
Preggie Pop Drops 13
Carlee & Cohen 15
"For I Know the Plans I Have for You" 18
Babymooning in California 20
"My Princess, I Have Set You Apart" 22
"Girls are Taking Over the World!" 24
Kicks and Giggles 27
Buenos Noches Luna & Pink Jungle Jill 30
"My Princess, You Are My Masterpiece" 32
The Touchpoint 33
What to Expect When You're NOT Expecting to Be Expecting 36
Chocolate Diapers 38
All in His Good and Perfect Time 41
"What's in Your Belly?" 44
Mother's Day 47
Home Sweet Home 50
Dreaming of Peanut 52
"You're Lucky" 55
Love Covers It All 58

Stork Parking	61
Bringing the Hidden into the Light	63
Guess that Bump	67
Babies Have FINGERNAILS!	70
Bigfoot Birthday	72
"A Brook Would Lose its Song if God Removed the Rocks"	75
Hiccups	77
God is Not Surprised	79
Good Things Come in Small Packages	83
The Home Stretch	86
My Reality	90
This is the Day that the Lord has Made	93
A Mother's Love	96
Baby Blues	100
Squeaker	103
Let Go and Let God	106
Living in the Moment	108
Simple Pleasures	111
The Terrible, Awful, Good-for-Nothing Car Seat	115
Bump in the Road	118
Baby Talk	121
On Wings Like Eagles	123
A Different "Forever" Kind of Love	126
Just Keep Swimming, Swimming, Swimming	129
One Year Ago Today	132
This is My Story, This is My Song	136

Hope for Gabriel

"For nothing is impossible with God" (Luke 1:37). That's what the angel, Gabriel, said to Mary soon after he told her that she had the Son of God growing in her womb. I've heard that story every year as Christmas approaches, yet *not once* did I think of the significance of Gabriel's final words and how desperately Mary needed to hear them.

Not until November 29th, 2010.

My story starts a little differently, in that there was no bright, glowing angel assuring me of the baby growing within. My assurance came from a positive pregnancy test at a local crisis pregnancy center and one of the volunteer counselors who worked there. Although Mary's story wasn't the first thing that came to mind, I can relate to her now, as that was the most helpless and afraid that I have ever felt. As a 21-year-old junior in college, I would have given anything for a glowing angel to reassure me that this seemingly impossible truth would be made possible through God. Instead, I was filled with shame and fear and anger at what I had done to my life and my future.

My "impossible" was happening.

However, when the counselor asked me what my plans were for the baby, I was more confident in that moment than I have ever been. Although I had made a mistake that would forever change the plans I so deeply desired for my future, God had already begun to use that mistake to delicately create a miracle within me. Without a doubt, I chose life and God began to change mine.

Its Heart is Already Beating

"Although it is very, very small, its heart is already beating . . . ." Among the many other words the crisis pregnancy center counselor, Susie, shared with the father (Mateo) and me, those were the most astonishing. As a biology major, I should have known more about the process of fetal development, but what she told me still amazed me as if it were the first time I had ever heard it.

Susie walked me through a book of pictures progressing from conception and on (soon after informing me that I was now five weeks pregnant). The shock subsided a little as Susie helped me grasp the reality of the situation: God had started a life inside me and I was going to be a mom.

Susie also spent hours that day counseling Mateo and me, and advising us regarding what our next steps should be. The idea of sharing the news of my pregnancy with my family shot me right back into shame and fear. The next three days were the slowest of my life as I sought advice from my incredibly supportive college roommates. Together, we began praying desperately. I specifically prayed that God would prepare my parents' hearts for the news I would soon share with them and that He would give me the words to say.

From the start, I knew the only way I could possibly get through it was if God was in control. Several times I prayed and told Jesus, "If You're ready, feel free to come back today. I'm ready to go home!" Wouldn't that have been perfect timing?

I prayed and flipped through my Bible more than ever before, searching for anything and everything that could bring me comfort. Several Bible verses suddenly held much greater meaning for me. I prayed specifically over verses such as 1 Peter 4:8, "Above all, love each other deeply, because love covers over a multitude of sins." I've never doubted my family's love for me, so that verse reaffirmed for me that even this circumstance wouldn't change their love.

When the time came for me to tell my family, although nervous, I had already grown leaps and bounds in my faith through my dependence on the Lord for strength, direction, and comfort. My roommates constantly reminded me of God's presence and His love for me. God was making it clearer to me than ever that with Him all things are possible.

My best friend, Claire, drove me to Roanoke to meet with my parents. She and I prayed together one last time before meeting with my parents to share the news. The details of that meeting are not as important as the outcome: my parents' love for me *MORE* than covered my multitude of sins. They were, as expected, shocked and upset. However, they were very quick to forgive and begin comforting me in my darkest hour.

The next few weeks were full of processing, healing, and family discussions. As our family trip to Israel was approaching, we knew God was about to do huge things at a time when we really needed Him as a family. I somehow made it through the last few weeks of my fall semester and anxiously awaited standing in the place where Mary was informed that she, too, had a second heartbeat.

Driving for Three

As my mom and I made the drive to Lynchburg, Virginia to share the news with my younger brother, Matthew, my nervousness and shame were quick to return. The fact that I had NO idea how he would react was what scared me the most. I have, from Day One, been that overly protective big sister trying very hard to be a good role model. (I partially blame that on my parents for telling me that he was "my baby," to avoid any jealousy.) The last thing I wanted to do was tell my younger brother that I had failed him as a good role model.

My mom and I had it all planned out. He would be waiting for us at his apartment with his girlfriend. I would take him to his room and tell him, as my mom shared the news with her. And so it went. Although surprised and angry at first, Matthew was *so* quick to comfort and encourage me. And by quick, I really do mean quick . . . like five minutes quick. He reassured me that this didn't change the way he looked at me, and that he loved me just the same.

Toward the end of our short conversation, he even joked about soon being the "best uncle ever." We ended the night by going to eat dinner all together. Matthew has always been the comic relief of our family. It doesn't take much effort on his part to have us all laughing so hard we cry. Admittedly, I worried during dinner that I had hurt Matthew somehow, or forever changed him. But I soon realized he was very much the same. When we left the restaurant, we hugged and said our goodbyes. As Matthew hugged my mom, I turned just in time to hear him say, "Be careful Mom. Now you're driving for three."

Healing in the Holy Land

As I settled back in at home, reality began to set in. I had less work to do, which left me with more time to think. I continued to remind my family and myself that when God presents you with a tough situation, He simultaneously gives you the strength to get through it. On top of being pregnant, I had also landed myself in what seemed to be the middle of an emotional battlefield. I fought constant negative emotions and thoughts about the pregnancy. Being at home had a different feel now, with an ever-present elephant in the room.

Though their love for me never wavered and they were quick to support and care for me, every day was still a reminder of my family's struggles to process the pregnancy and what it meant for my future. I also struggled as I found myself "walking on egg shells," avoiding at all costs any conversation that might further upset my family or me. This only led to a buildup of feelings that I couldn't comfortably express. I quickly realized how unhealthy this was becoming for me emotionally and once again set my eyes upon the Lord for guidance.

Never having dealt with such intense emotions, I knew I needed to seek further Christian guidance and support. Many gracious friends of the family were willing to meet with me and offer me wise words of encouragement. I met with two pastors and a counselor before leaving for Israel with my family. There were a lot of emotions that I wanted to diminish before heading to the Holy Land. It was important to me that once I left with my family, I could fully focus on what God was trying to show me.

When we arrived in Israel, one of our very first destinations was none other than the "Church of the Annunciation"—a church built where Gabriel confronted Mary with the news of her unplanned pregnancy. In this sacred place, my family gathered around me to pray. The first step of our healing from God.

We were also blessed with the ability to see the place where Jesus was born. Just as the many people before me, I knelt for a moment to touch it. In that instant, I could only think of Mary. How scared she must have been. How unsure she must have felt about her future. And most importantly, how her strength and confidence that came from the Lord had blessed her beyond belief!

We experienced many more healing moments on that trip. For me, personally, there was a miraculous healing of "morning sickness." Up until the trip, I had experienced that lovely symptom daily. But from the morning we left until ten days later when we returned, I did not get sick once. This may have been from my ability to avoid the interesting, but not so pregnancy-friendly food of the Middle East. After all, who wants to eat hummus and fish that much anyway?

But back to the point: Our time in Israel was the beginning of a shower of blessings from God. For example, God (being the Master Planner) had divinely placed a very special couple on the trip with us. A man and his wife in our group had gone through the exact same experience when their daughter discovered she was pregnant soon before her high school graduation.

I knew God wanted me to talk to the mother and I anxiously awaited His timing. Although later than expected, His timing came perfectly. We talked for hours in the airport in France during our five-hour layover on the way home. I shared with her my story and my emotions about the pregnancy, which rushed back the instant we began talking. She was able to shed light on the parents' side of the pregnancy and what that process looked like for them. Until that point, I had not realized how different my parents' healing would be from my own. It was such an encouragement to hear from a mother that she had survived the struggle, healed from the pain, and now can't imagine her life without her grandson.

These blessings, among many others, sparked the beginning of some truly divine healing. At the time, I never expected things to start moving so quickly.

Peanut Wants Waffles

Once my family made our 17-hour expedition back to the United States, life in the "real world" started back up. More specifically, my "mornafternightime" sickness started again. And that's exactly what it was! There was really no point in eating anything EVER because it wasn't long before I had the pleasure of revisiting that meal.

In the beginning, I made many attempts to conceal my disgusting symptom so as not to set off a domino effect of family nausea (we're all pretty sensitive to the sound of being sick). But I soon found that my family, although I'm sure preferred not to hear it, were concerned enough that they wanted to help in any way they could. One morning I had just finished my last bite when I felt it coming right back. As I made my way to the bathroom, mom was quick to follow to help me. My brother and my dad made the best of the rest of their breakfast, drowning out the noise by singing loudly. I'm not sure what's worse—actually throwing up, or trying to throw up while laughing.

In the beginning of January, reality hit once again when I went in for my first ultrasound. Mateo and I went together to see the little one for the first time and hear the sweetest sound ever: the heartbeat! I was ten weeks along at this point and didn't know much about ultrasounds. All I expected was a little white dot and some swooshing sounds. But to our surprise, the baby was a little over an inch in length and way more distinct than a dot!

The woman doing the ultrasound pointed out the various features: eyes, ears, torso, legs, etc. She then proceeded to push and wiggle the device on my tummy while saying, "Wake up! Wake up!" My first reaction was, "Yeah right, it can't move already." But once again, my biology knowledge failed me and I'll be darned if that little fetus didn't go to town stretching and kicking and throwing out all the tricks for us to see! God must have known I needed extra convincing that I really was carrying a little life.

My family was anxiously waiting at home to see the pictures and hear about the ultrasound. I shared with them about the cute tricks the baby had already begun to perform without me even knowing. When my brother asked me, "How big is it?" I replied, "About the size of a peanut" . . . and it stuck. My brother, along with the rest of my family, would probably forever call him or her "Peanut."

Days went on and the nausea only got worse, but I discovered that the cure was contained in a childhood favorite food of mine: waffles! Pop one of those Eggo's in the toaster and eat it plain! That was the only food little Peanut would let me keep down, so I went with it. My roommates got quite a laugh out of the huge stock of waffles I had stored up in our freezer. Better than pickles and ice cream, I suppose!

Preggie Pop Drops

I was overwhelmed by the tremendous outpouring of love and support I received from friends, family, and people I didn't even know. My extended family (cousins, aunts, and grandparents) were quick to remind me how much they love me. Telling anyone close to me about my pregnancy was a real struggle at first because of my prideful desire to keep up a certain image of myself, but I was slowly realizing that God was creating a new, beautiful image in me.

My mom jumped right into gear and started a prayer group of wonderful women. She sent weekly emails updating them on anything new and asking for specific prayer requests. Prayer is a powerful thing. Having only known about my pregnancy for three months at that stage, the number of prayers that God had already answered amazed me. Every week we received advice, encouraging Bible verses, and support from many of the women. This, along with encouragement from others, helped give us strength and direction into the joy God calls us to have in hard circumstances.

For me, the start of that joy came the day before I left to go back to school. My mom and dad and I went downtown to have breakfast on the market (which was delicious the first time). I was still having a hard time with morning sickness, and it was beginning to weigh me down. On a whim right after breakfast, Mom and I decided to go to a children's consignment shop just to look around. But looking turned into excited planning and brainstorming about bedroom themes and baby items. We decided to continue our extravaganza by heading to a toy store, where we spent two hours marveling at all the innovative things available for babies now. It's a good thing we didn't know the sex of the baby yet, because quite a pretty penny would have been spent that day.

To finish the day, we then went to a maternity store to purchase my first maternity outfit. Having just lost 20 pounds prior to getting pregnant, I was not too thrilled with the idea of getting big. Mom and I together came to accept that reality as I put on the Velcro pregnant belly pillow underneath one of the shirts I tried on. I remember not knowing whether I should laugh or be serious, until mom suggested we take a picture. I, of course, nipped that idea in the bud, but was relieved to see my mom finding humor in some of it.

As we paid for my new bellyband, jeans, and shirts, Mom found a small container of "Preggie Pop Drops." According to the woman at the counter, they were an all-natural solution to morning sickness. At this point, I would have tried anything. But no need to look further because those suckers worked! It was at least another three weeks before I got sick again. Those little candies saved me more than a few times in my Entomology (insect) lab—like the day we had to dissect a very unfortunate grasshopper.

Carlee & Cohen

By eighteen weeks pregnant, I felt miles ahead of where I was in the beginning. God blessed me with such an incredible family and circle of friends, all of whom helped me through what I consider to be the hardest time of my life. After many weekends back home spent with the family, we all grew as a whole to be joyful about the blessing that this life really is. We frequently talked about Peanut and the excitement we felt for his or her future. Mateo's family was also an incredible encouragement to me. Most of his family still lived in Colombia, but when his mom, Claudia, visited recently, her family showed an overflowing love and excitement for me and the baby. I, of course, was thrilled with the idea that my child would have two loving families. Also, with my newly acquired Spanish skills (after spending the summer in Spain), I was so excited that my child would have the opportunity to be bilingual from the start!

In the past, when I would dream about my future family, I had almost every detail planned out. I thank my mom for my constant desire to plan ahead. For the first 18 years of my life, I watched as she planned ahead for every intricate detail of our day-to-day schedules, weekends, vacations, etc. So, for years I knew that I wanted to name my first daughter Carlee and my first son Cohen. I can't recall where those names came from, but they stuck with me and my dreams for a long time. But once I actually had to plan a reality instead of a dream, those names lost their sparkle. Instead I found myself constantly listening to names or reading them, hoping to hear that perfect one. It was a little scary when I thought about it. God had given me the incredible responsibility to decide the ONE name of thousands that my child would be called for the rest of his or her life. This name could be used for so many things in the future—the name on the birth certificate, the name family and friends would use to catch his or her attention, the name read over a loud speaker to win an award or join the principal for some disciplinary fun, the name that would be written on every application, identification, paper, etc., the name that would one day make another boy or girl's heart flutter. Such an important thing a name is! How would I ever decide?

Luckily, I was able to come up with a short list. However, some important details applied: if the baby was a boy, the middle name would be Matthew, after my brother and my grandfather—so the first name *had* to fit with Matthew. If it was a girl, I wanted to be able to incorporate Anne somehow. For the many years that I loved the name Carlee, I loved how it sounded with the middle name Anne, which is also my Nana's first name. Since Carlee was no longer on my list of favorites, I found other interesting ways to incorporate "Anne." For example, "Annabel Lily" or "Adrianna Grace." The second was my favorite because Grace was Mateo's grandmother's name. Unfortunately, I struggled to find a name I liked that sounded just right for a boy and rolled off the tongue with "Matthew." I found this a little funny, since I had the hunch all along that the baby would be a boy. Because of my recent love for the name Adrianna, I considered the name Adrian Matthew. But . . . although I am notorious for planning ahead, I also have the terrible habit of repeatedly changing my mind! Just two more weeks until we know, pink or blue?!

My guess?

Blue.

"For I Know the Plans I Have for you"

"...plans for you to prosper, not to harm you. Plans to give you a hope and a future" (Jeremiah 29:11). This Bible verse, amongst many others, gave me a lot of comfort during my pregnancy. It was a huge help in reminding me daily that, although this was lightyears away from any plan I had for my future, God clearly had other plans.

One lesson I learned quite frequently in college is how God's plan always trumps mine. Regardless of how convinced I may be about what is best for my life or what may bring me the greatest joy, I have repeatedly learned that God's plan always plays out with the greatest outcome, even when it seems like His path is painful or hard. We can't see the forest for the trees. The forest I found myself in seemed pretty big and dense—but God continually guided me through it.

As mentioned earlier, before any of this happened, I had my whole forest mapped out in my mind, tree for tree. My biggest goal was medical school. I never lost sight of that goal in the midst of my pregnancy, but I surely saw it get farther and farther away. But once again, God knows His plans! I may have done fine on the MCAT's before, but being pregnant gave me a second wind of motivation to finish strong.

I'll admit, having to study for the MCAT's and take the test in the midst of my pregnancy was not ideal in my mind, but it must have been in God's! I prayed that God would be clear in His desires for my future and that my MCAT score would reflect more certainly if medical school was the best direction for me.

Lo and behold, I received a score of 29. That may not mean a lot to you, but it was a much better score than I had anticipated or even wanted (I was aiming for 27). Receiving that high of a score felt like God had put up a billboard in my forest that read, "I may rearrange your plans, but I don't always change them."

Another exciting development during this time was my parent's decision about what they would like the baby to call them. My dad chose the name "Pappy." At first, my mom wanted to match Pappy and have the name "Nanny," however, she got a little more creative and decided to go with "Laney," a spin-off of her middle name, "Lane." It was definitely weird thinking about my parents being grandparents, but then I remembered it was even weirder to realize I would soon be a mom . . . and then it all seemed right, because it was. God had it written in His big ol' book of "Me" before I was even born. Which only makes me wonder: *What amazing plans does He already have set in place for the future of my child?*

Babymooning in California

A few months before finding out I was pregnant, I planned to spend my Spring Break doing medical missions with Haitian orphans in the Dominican Republic, just as I had done the previous year. I anxiously awaited my return trip to the DR after God put a tremendous passion in my heart for the people and children there. I had worked hard to recruit students to go on International Service Learning trips as I had done, in order to gain "credits" toward another trip. Finally, just a few weeks before my unexpected surprise, I had raised enough credits for a free trip: Spring Break! But going to a third world country to work with people facing serious illnesses and infections was not conducive to a pregnancy. After painfully giving up that trip, God opened the door for me to go to Sacramento, California with my mom. We made plans to stay with some of my dearest friends, who were really more like family. When I was in high school, I spent a summer as a nanny for their son, Alexander, while they welcomed their new baby girl, Avery.

I grew very attached to the family through that experience, and could now say that God used that summer (a whopping five years earlier) to prepare me for the upcoming year. I learned so much about parenting and what it takes to raise and take care of a child. I also experienced some of the greatest gifts of parenting. For example, I learned how to deeply cherish every minute of cuddling a toddler while he slowly falls asleep.

Needless to say, I fell in love with their children and have continued to delight in their growth over the years. They are just one of the great examples of how God was preparing me before I could even fathom what was planned!

After a whirlwind weekend of packing and preparing, Mom and I set out to California for what we soon began to call "The Babymoon." The family we stayed with explained that a babymoon is like a honeymoon, only before the main event! And oh, what a great babymoon it was! Mom and I spent a day shopping around Sacramento, exploring their multitude of baby paraphernalia. We spent a day in Napa, exploring the countryside and vineyards and enjoying each other's company. We also spent a day in San Francisco, seeing all the main sights and making the most of an awesome mother-daughter trip. We spent as much of our free time as possible with our hosts, doting on their sweet family. The week as a whole was exactly what I needed—a week AWAY in a new, exciting place to further process and anticipate the next big transition in my life.

My new appreciation for God's unexpected plans came in handy as Mom and I discovered we missed our flight home by an entire day! Although aggravating at first, we soon realized that this mishap gave us a much-needed extra day with our friends and with each other. We couldn't for the life of us figure out how such a mistake could be made, but I've learned that when the unexplainable happens, the only explanation is God. So, we absorbed every last minute of California and headed home the next day.

"My Princess, I Have Set You Apart"

The following excerpt comes from the book, *His Princess: Love Letters from Your King*, by Sheri Rose Shepherd:

I have called you to be set apart, just as I called those who came before you. I know this calling will sometimes come with great cost, but the eternal rewards are priceless and beyond comparison. Just as I did with Queen Esther, I have given you the ability to walk in such a way so all will see that you are divinely Mine. Some will admire you for your dedication to Me, and some will want you to fail rather than follow My lead. You may fall because you are not perfect, but your mistakes can be the tutors that make you wiser. Don't put pressure on yourself to be perfect. I'm the only one who can perfect you, My princess. All I ask is that you let Me set you apart so that I use you as a witness for the world to see.

Love,
Your King, who sets you apart

"I knew you before I formed you in your mother's womb. Before you were born *I set you apart* and appointed you as my spokesman to the world." – Jeremiah 1:5, emphasis mine

"Girls are Taking Over the World!"

Up until the day of my ultrasound when we would finally learn the baby's gender,

whenever anyone would say they thought the baby was a girl, I would simply smile while thinking "Wrong . . . it's a boy. I just feel it." This, of course, was my "hunch" as an expecting mother, so no way could I be wrong . . . .

Well, the ultrasound thought otherwise. As I sat there, looking at a baby-shaped black and white blob, the ultrasound technician very nonchalantly explained that due to the lack of a certain missing protrusion between the legs, this baby is a girl. I knew either way I would be excited, but my first reaction was, "What?! I was wrong?! Bring on years of terrible mother instincts . . . ."

The ultrasound continued and the doctor pointed out all the little developing organs, working just as they were supposed to. She switched it over to 3-D viewing at one point and was able to show us the baby's face. I, of course, thought she was beautiful already. The technician seemed to think my girl would be a drama queen, due to her lack of cooperation with the ultrasound. Apparently the baby didn't really want us to see her that well, because she continued to stay turned away from the view with her fist over her face for most of the time. It was only a matter of time, however, before she began throwing elbows in what I think was frustration at us for intruding in her already limited space. This short period allowed us to see her little face, details and all.

When the ultrasound was over, I was thrilled and anxious to share the news. Mateo and I first shared the news with his family over speakerphone. They were *so* excited, especially since they had been hoping for a girl all along. I then rushed home to share the news with my family. I had prepared a small box with a can of peanuts that I had decorated pink. I placed the DVD of the ultrasound inside and carefully explained all that I could remember to my brother, my mother, and my dad. They then opened the box to find my little surprise and were ecstatic! Matthew immediately began bragging about how he had known all along while excitedly congratulating and hugging me. My dad exclaimed, "That's what I wanted! A little you! A mini you!"

This news was surprising to me, because he was the only one who hadn't said what he thought the baby would be. My mom, through tears of joy, hugged me and gave me the most adorable little girl outfit to start what I was sure would soon be a collection of little baby clothes. She then proceeded to text and email the masses. I called my grandparents and quickly texted my friend we had stayed with in California. She responded with congratulations and a brief story of her children's response to the news. Her daughter, Avery, immediately decided she wanted to draw a picture of my baby. Alexander, however, took it a little differently. He burst into huge tears and exclaimed, "I knew it! I knew it! Girls are taking over the world!" From the mouths of babes!

I then made plans to share the news with my roommates and close friends. I baked some cookies with pink icing on top and covered them all individually with foil. I then gave one to each of them and asked them to open it after watching the DVD. The majority of them also thought it was a girl from the get-go and all of them were very excited.

Honestly, I began the day feeling pretty nervous about learning the gender of my child. Each steps in the journey pushed me a little more into reality—especially this one! I already knew that God had a lot of life lessons planned out for me to learn through this little girl. As a female myself, I knew from experience that life is not all pretty and pink. I felt excited but also nervous to see what kind of experiences my daughter would go through. I knew God had equipped me to guide her through some of her future, but at the same time, I knew there would also be many experiences I may know nothing about. I hoped and prayed that God would grant me the wisdom for those situations. And I prayed to God she didn't get my middle school attitude!

Kicks and Giggles

Feeling your baby kick for the first time is supposed to be this momentous, possibly emotional moment. Some moms cry, others may excitedly run to tell others, and still others may sigh because it is definitely a moment of relief when you can finally feel your baby move and know everything is okay. Me, however . . . I giggled.

The first time was late at night. I was lying in bed with my mind lost in that thoughtless period right after praying and before dozing off. Then, I felt it—what my mom had described to be a "fluttering" feeling in my lower stomach. I thought many times before that I felt her move, but this time I knew it was real, and I giggled—consistently, for a good five minutes as she continued to kick, wiggle, squirm, and whatever else she may have been doing. The little "diva" (as my roommates started to call her) made a habit of these late night parties. I'm wasn't sure what she could possibly be dancing about. Perhaps the delicious dinner I made? Perhaps she already had rhythm and was using my heartbeat as her song? Or maybe she was just enjoying her newly discovered ability to use my bladder as a punching bag. Either way, she went to town!

A lucky few were around for my baby girl's late night party habits and felt her little spurts. My mom and brother were the first, followed by my roommates. Although she usually got going late at night, she most definitely didn't stop there. I even noticed a song or two on one of my

CD's that really got her moving. Either that, or she already hated my singing and kicking and elbowing me was her way of trying to get me to shut up! She also hated one pair of jeans I was still trying to wear. The buttons, even when unbuttoned, apparently pressed a little too tightly for my diva, and as we saw in the ultrasound, she hated for her space to be intruded upon.

Although I refrained from giggling when sharing the exciting moment with others, I still giggled whenever I experienced it alone. I'm not sure if it was because it was a bit funny to feel something strange moving uncontrollably inside your body, or because I felt so many emotions at once that the only release was through a laugh. I definitely enjoyed every kick, wiggle, and squirm. Not only because the movements assured me that the baby was doing all right in there, but also because she was constantly reminding me of her presence. That's not to say that I forgot, because ever since finding out I was pregnant, I could think of very few moments when the reality had left my mind. But it seemed as if with every kick, she was reminding me that she was very real and that God had a purpose and plan for her tiny yet quickly growing life.

Not many people knew the details of the week before I found out about my pregnancy. That week was full of reasons why my daughter shouldn't exist. The weekend before and the week of Thanksgiving, I consumed enough wine to worry most pregnant mothers. That Monday, I woke to a nasty case of strep throat and was quickly prescribed a strong antibiotic, which I took religiously for days. It was the week of Thanksgiving, so my stress level was higher than normal due to the holiday and preparing for visiting family. On top of it all, a very close friend of mine died in a hiking accident, causing a whirlwind of intense shock, depression, and denial. The night before I found out I was pregnant, I had driven a few hours with close friends to go to the funeral which was, needless to say, very emotional.

All of those circumstances are generally avoided in the very beginning of pregnancy, due to the huge risks of miscarriage so early on. Because of all this, I could confidently say I believe God has a very real purpose for my daughter's existence, as He does for every one of His children. Although I may have considered her to be "unplanned," God considers her entirely *planned*, from conception to eternal life. And with every kick and giggle, I got a reminder of how determined He was to have her present in my life, fulfilling that unpredictable plan.

Buenos Noches Luna & Pink Jungle Jill

Remember the children's book, *Goodnight Moon*? What a classic! I was thrilled to that little gem in Spanish, called *Buenos Noches Luna*. I decided to start reading it aloud every night, along with two of my other favorite childhood books: *Eres Mi Mamá? (Are You My Mother?)* by Dr. Seuss, and *Siempre Te Querré (I'll Love You Forever)* by Robert Munsch. A wise mother-friend of mine told me that after reading one book consistently to her first child while pregnant with her second, she found that her second child was soothed by her reading that book.

I reasoned that if I started rocking in a rocking chair every night around the same time while reading the same books consistently, maybe—just maybe—I could get my little diva on a semi-sleeping schedule before she was even born. Ha! I knew it would be a lucky chance, but figured it was worth a try.

I learned from my *What to Expect When You're Expecting* reading that by 23 weeks, my daughter already had the ability to experience REM sleep—which meant she could have dreams! My brother's comment was, "Of what, the darkness?"

I imagined she may be dreaming of swinging around by the umbilical cord, or doing a little break dance on my bladder or swimming from one side to the other (which consisted of significantly less space than she had before). Maybe she was dreaming of those earlier days when she could freely roam around.

Around this time, the bedding for the baby's crib arrived. After much searching, I settled on an adorable, girlie, jungle-themed pattern called "Jungle Jill." To prevent entirely "pink-ifying" my life again, I decided to balance out the pink with some brown. The previous year, my friends teased me about the amount of pink I had incorporated into my clothes, furniture, etc. Not long before discovering the diva, I gave up my pink ways and shifted to a more "mature" color scheme—but I secretly looked forward to enjoying the color pink vicariously through my sweet girl.

"My Princess, You Are My Masterpiece"

From my special book . . .

I love what I have created. I am delighted in you! Don't ever feel insecure about what you think you are not, because I made you in My image and your uniqueness is a gift from Me. I did not give you a life, My love, for you to squeeze into a man-made mold. You are royalty, but you won't discover that truth by gazing into a mirror. Let Me be your mirror and I will reflect back to you your true beauty. The more you gaze at Me, the more you will see My workmanship in you. The sooner you see yourself for who you really are, the sooner you can begin your reign as My priceless princess with a PURPOSE.

Love, your King and your Creator

"For we are God's masterpiece, He created us anew in Christ Jesus so that we can do the good things he planned for us long ago." – Ephesians 2:10

The Touchpoint

Ever since my mom began playing in her contemporary worship band, "Touchpoint," she enthusiastically explained the meaning of the name to anyone who would listen. A "touchpoint" is the place where the branch of a grapevine meets the central vine. She related this to the well-known Bible verse, "I am the vine and you are the branches. If a man remains in me, and I in Him, he will bear much fruit. For without me you can do nothing" (John 5:15).

From a science viewpoint, the touchpoint is essential—it's where all of the branch gets its nutrients for growth and life. It joins the tiny vessels to the main "pipeline." Cutting off that connection prevents any and all growth entirely. In the verse, John is referring to our spiritual connection to the One True Vine: God. He is our supplier of "nutrients" for spiritual growth and a "fruit-producing" life. As a Christian, I have heard this metaphor enough times to be desensitized to its importance. Although I see the word "touchpoint" frequently among my mother's belongings and even hear sermons and references to this verse, I had shut off my sensitivity to the deeper meaning. That is, until one night at a Cru (Campus Crusade) event.

Several students and a leader stood up to give their testimonies. All the testimonies were moving, and a great reminder of how blessed I was, even in my toughest circumstances. One testimony included a reference to that verse about the vine, but the way the speaker worded it reopened my eyes to a part of the verse that often gets overshadowed: "without me you can do nothing." The speaker said, "As a branch, it is not your job to try your hardest to squeeze out a fruit. If you are focused on staying connected to the branch, the fruit comes naturally."

In my previous understanding of that verse, there was a branch connected to a vine that provided nutrients so that the branch could work hard and use the nutrients perfectly to produce the best fruit. However, when relating this to my spiritual life, I realized I was giving myself impossible expectations. I was trying hard to perfectly produce the fruit: "love, joy, peace, patience, kindness, goodness, faithfulness, gentleness, and self-control" (Galatians 5:22), along with strength, stability, and understanding. I would pray diligently for patience and often received divine provision in trying situations . . . for about a week!

I would then realize my peace was out of whack, so I focused on peace and then my other "fruit" would suffer—an endless cycle of failure. I was constantly trying to squeeze out the perfect fruit, to take control of my own uncontrollable life and situation, and create what I believed to be best. But by taking control myself, it only caused me worry, stress, and self-doubt. The longer I focused on controlling my own production of fruit, the less I focused on where my nutrients, strength, and life came from.

What a relief that we all have our own personal touchpoint to the Provider of the fruit—the One in complete control of our growth! For me more personally, what a relief to know that with every step of pregnancy and motherhood, I am not expected to handle it alone, using my own strength. As I continued through this rollercoaster of a journey, God constantly provided me with all that I needed to endure it, whether it felt like it in the moment or not. Rather than focusing on fixing all of the problems or making important decisions independently, if I focus entirely on my touchpoint to God, my fruit will blossom naturally as a result. Without a touchpoint to the Father, I can do nothing.

What to Expect When You're NOT Expecting to Be Expecting

My mother was very quick to buy me the famous book, *What to Expect When You're Expecting*. In fact, I think she purchased it within 24 hours of learning about my pregnancy. At first, I felt very uncomfortable reading it because it forced me into the reality of accepting my life change. But as the weeks went by, I became absolutely fascinated by the amazing facts it provided about my baby girl. Each week, she was the size of a new fruit or food item. I can still remember the week she was the size of an orange seed and I thought that was so big! But that is small compared to her growing body at just over a pound at Week 24. According to the book, at 24 weeks she was able to feel me dancing, so I incorporated some new dance routines into my day. Then I realized that it was probably not a pleasant feeling to be jostled around in a tight, dark space with no idea why.

The book also provided amazing insight on new symptoms I may experience and the incredible things my body was doing each month. However, the book didn't include a list of potentially uncomfortable situations that may come along with an unexpected pregnancy. This is why I think someone could make quite a bit of money publishing a book called, "What to Expect When You're NOT Expecting to Be Expecting."

For example, when you are NOT expecting a pregnancy, you should be prepared for the range of reactions you will receive from different people. I can distinctly remember the first time I got an excited, congratulatory reaction. I was so blown away by it, although relieved. But I remember feeling guilty for getting a positive reaction. Also, the book may include a section on how to handle the unexpected pregnancy while continuing with your academic or business life. It is obviously not ideal to be in school while pregnant, and I think there are many reasons for that. However, being pregnant while at school does has a few perks! For example, while pregnant I had my very important Pre-Med interview with the Health Advising Committee. I was a nervous wreck and spent a lot of time dreading the thought of not knowing the answer to an important question. However, during one of the very first interview questions, my little diva gave me what I think were some encouraging "You can do it, Mommy!" kicks and wiggles. Feeling her presence relaxed me a little and I finished the interview with flying colors.

Although I was not expecting to be expecting, I was daily amazed by how God was already preparing me for this time in my life long before I knew about it. A lot of the biological "mother-instinct" parts of me definitely kicked in, but at the same time, there was also a deeper preparation I was completely unaware of. God is, after all, the master of unplanned pregnancies.

Chocolate Diapers

I was continually reminded of how intricately planned all of this was by God. It became clear to me that God was incredibly intentional about who He would use to help me through my last year at Virginia Tech. I've always felt blessed by the friends I've had while away from family and living at school, but my final year was different for a variety of reasons.

God knew I would need friends who could encourage me and carry me through the toughest times. I don't know why being pregnant initially made me feel unloved, but I know it stemmed from the feeling that I didn't deserve the love and respect I had received by everyone before being pregnant. It didn't take long at all for God to reassure me that despite my past, I was still loved by those close to me. My roommates started it all. They were immediately encouraging and prayerful when they found out I was pregnant. From there, my family and more close friends jumped right in, enthusiastic to help in any way they could, all the while loving me for who I was and always had been.

A few friends planned and organized my very first baby shower. Honestly, I was mostly nervous about it. I couldn't wrap my mind around having my closest friends with me celebrating my unplanned pregnancy. But once the party started and everyone was there, it was clear to me that they were all there to celebrate the creation of life, only made possible by God. I couldn't believe the overflowing excitement and love they had for my daughter and me.

My baby shower was a bit unconventional. I intentionally invited some of my close guy friends. I was worried they may feel uncomfortable with all of it, but everyone handled it incredibly well. My roommates and one of my close friends planned, organized, and catered the entire event! They made baby pigs in a blanket, hamburger sliders, fruit and veggie platters, chips and dip, and adorable homemade pink iced cupcakes!

They also organized some games to get everyone excited, the first of which I had never heard of. There were five numbered diapers, each of which contained a different melted chocolate candy bar. The diapers were then passed around as people tried to guess which candy bar had been melted in each one. It was *hilarious*! Everyone was cracking up as the diapers were peeled open to reveal very mushy brown chocolate. Some even resorted to tasting the mystery element in an attempt to guess what it was. I laughed so hard it hurt, all the while in awe of how blessed I was to have the friends I do. They enthusiastically participated in several games and watched as I opened their thoughtful gifts. I couldn't help but think of how showered in love my daughter was already. So many of her belongings will be gifts given out of love for her! A popular gift was swaddling blankets. Several of the guys expressed curiosity about the process of swaddling. This led to a hilarious attempt by one of my roommates to swaddle one of the guys in a big pink blanket! I hadn't laughed that hard in a long, long time.

It was amazing to me the way God makes sure to show you love when you need it. I think it's a natural response to feel guilty and undeserving when you are shown incredible love, but for me, that baby shower was such a reminder of what Christ's love looks like—completely unconditional, forever overflowing, and utterly amazing. It was such a blessing to know that my friends, family, and God loved my daughter and me this way, before she was even born.

All in His Good and Perfect Time

It was hard to describe how weird it felt to approach graduation and parenthood at the same time. While all of my friends faced challenges like, "What job should I apply for?" or "Where do I want to live?" or "Where will I travel first?", I faced decisions like, "What car seat is safest?" and "Cloth or disposable diapers?" I also focused hard on decisions for medical school, but I found that decisions about my daughter consumed my thoughts far more frequently. It was no longer a surprise to me that I sometimes felt envious of my friends as they made their plans for the future. That was a consequence I faced almost immediately after discovering I was pregnant. It felt as if every week, there was another couple getting engaged or someone landing the job they had worked so hard for. Graduation became a frequent topic of discussion and it was hard not to think of how my dreams of post-graduation life used to look much more similar to my friends' futures, entering the real world with independence and freedom and a plethora of decisions to make, all while building an exciting new future.

In God's grace, I had to sacrifice very few future plans, but adding a child to the mix changed everything drastically. Whereas before I would have spent quite a bit of time only considering my wants and desires for my future, I now also had to focus a lot of attention on what would be best for my daughter. There were so many "real world" choices I knew I would be making, but making decisions about a child, *my* child, multiplied that pressure infinitely. I sometimes doubted my ability to handle it all and often asked God, "Why would You give this to me, and why at such a time as this?"

What a humbling answer God gives! Not only does He give us difficult circumstances in life, but He also provides the means for handling them. The Bible is full of instances where the same question could be asked: "Why now?" One example is the story of Abraham and Sarah. After years and years of praying and being faithful to God, finally at age 99 they were blessed with children. Although their situation was quite the opposite of mine, I couldn't help but relate to Sarah. She had to have been thinking, "What the heck, God? Why now?" along with a lot of excitement, I'm sure. I also think of the Easter story. Jesus knew His purpose was to save us all, as did His disciples, friends, and followers. But they must have been questioning God's timing when Jesus was led to Calvary. The people who had just heard Him preach and had a thirst for more of His teaching had to be asking, "Why at such a time as this?" But just as with the stories from Scripture, God's timing is never wrong. His answers to prayer come at the most perfect time in order to glorify Him.

So why should my story be any different? I know my daughter's existence is no mistake. Her life is a blessing, from beginning to end, with a purpose I may never fully understand. The fact that her existence began when it did may be a mystery and struggle to me, but I pushed forward in confidence that God is literally the Man with the plan. He is the Creator of time, so who am I to question His timing? In fact, God has to be answering, "What more perfect timing than right now?"

"What's in Your Belly?"

By about 25 weeks, no matter how big or baggy my clothes were, it became impossible for me to hide my pregnancy. For a while, I thought it would be a lot better once the bump was obviously a baby and not just some extra weight I was packing. At least then people could get instant confirmation, rather than stare during moments of curiosity. At first, that was how I could tell who knew. When I wasn't showing at all, a select few couldn't control their curiosity and spent the majority of our conversation time sneaking quick peeks at my stomach. Being oversensitive to it at the time, I was obviously very aware of their actions and wished my stomach was big enough to be seen by their more discreet peripheral vision.

But at 25 weeks along I was very obviously pregnant and it took very little staring to confirm it. But the staring only got worse. At first, I worried about the reactions I would get from students as they passed by me on the way to class. I had never seen a pregnant girl on campus that I was aware of, so I knew that I would stand out quite a bit. My mom was quick to calm my nerves about the staring, though. She very gently explained that most of the staring would be out of curiosity, not judgment. She and I related this back to my high school years when an upperclassman girl was pregnant. I can distinctly remember staring at her as she waddled down the hallway. Looking back I regretted my uncontrolled staring problem, but also remembered that my thoughts about her were never of judgment. I mostly just wondered how she felt or how hard that must have been for her. This became a comfort to me, realizing that most of the stares I received derived from curiosity and a desire to understand my situation.

My mom also helped me realize that some of the stares may have been spurred on by guilt. Abortions had become so available and common. I could only imagine how many girls that I passed daily may have faced the same decision I did, but chose the other option. In those cases, staring at me had an entirely different connotation. To them, I may have represented a choice they painfully regretted making. I could only hope and pray that the Lord would use my situation to give them the courage to seek comfort in the arms of Christ.

Some stares I didn't mind at all. I had been working as the Nursery Manager at my mother's church for the previous few months, specifically with the "5 and unders," who were still at the age when they had absolutely *no* discretion about what came out of their adorable little mouths. One Sunday, I was at the sink washing all the sippy cups from snack time as all the children circled around the television to watch a movie. One little boy came over and sat on the step stool right next to me, staring intently at my stomach and then my face. After a few moments of wondering why he had chosen to stare at me instead of an exciting VeggieTales movie, I said, "Hello, Robert." Kids will most often tell you exactly what they're thinking if you go about it the right way, and I really wanted to know what he was thinking. I could see the little wheels turning inside his head. He looked at me very seriously and asked, "What's in your belly?" I tried so hard not to laugh because I could tell he was very concerned with what I could possibly be smuggling under my shirt. So I told him, "Well, Robert, there's a baby girl growing in there." And without another thought, he asked, "Can I touch her?" as he reached out his little hands and gently placed them on my stomach.

This interaction was an incredible reminder of why God desires for us to seek a childlike faith. Not once have I felt nervous or uncomfortable about being obviously pregnant in front of children, mainly because they pass no judgment. My biggest fear was that people would stare and automatically think about the sin that created my blessing of a bump, rather than consider the miracle within. Many people have been quick to recognize God's goodness in all of it, but children instantly consider my bump with an innocent curiosity and excitement. It's such a great reminder to me that I should look at my situation the same way. Yes, it took sin to begin this hard and rocky journey, but through God's awesome power and love, that sin created a miracle. I prayed that God would help me look at my situation with the eyes of a child and see only the incomprehensible miracle of life growing in a fascinating bump beneath my shirt.

Mother's Day

As a "mom-to-be," I was pretty nervous about what Mother's Day would hold for me. I guess I didn't technically consider myself a mother yet, since my baby girl wasn't yet in the world for me to mother. I was especially anxious about how my family would celebrate Mother's Day, since I was finally home from school. Typically, Mother's Day in our family consisted of a day full of love, surprises, and gifts for Mom. Dad usually surprised her with a nice homemade meal including all her favorites. My brother and I typically put our heads together for a few days as we tried to decide what to get for her. After much debate, my brother was usually the one to think of the most thoughtful gift *ever*, and I would try to find something to complement it. Dad usually went for the logical gift, like something mom actually *needed*. He, of course, had an unfair advantage with gift-giving—as her husband, naturally he knew more about what she wanted.

This particular Mother's Day was different for several reasons. The most obvious difference was that there would now be one-and-a-half "mothers" in our house. Also, my brother was unable to make it home because he had two finals the next day, so there were no opportunities to team up on the gift-buying. This was also the first Mother's Day that I would be publicly pregnant at church. I naturally worry about things that maybe I shouldn't, so this posed a huge worry for me; I worried that some people would be debating whether or not to wish me a Happy Mother's Day. I love talking to people in general, so whether they said it or not would be no offense to me at all.

That morning, I quickly discovered that it was, to say the least, a little humorous the different ways that people approached it. I mostly got the straight up "Happy Mother's Day." I received an adorable card from one of my prayer warriors, and my mother had some of the ushers hunt me down at church to give me a Mother's Day rose. But the very first "Mother's Day" greeting I got was from my dad. He drove me to church, and as he dropped me off at the door, he said, "Happy Mother's Day, ya mudder" ('mudder' being his goofy way of saying 'mother'). Although his typical humor was added in, I knew it had to have been at least a little weird for him to say. Grasping the idea that your daughter will be a mother is probably never an easy thing to handle, especially with my situation—but realizing the challenge made his attempt all the more sweet, and it definitely broke the ice for what was sure to be many more "Happy Mother's Day" greetings.

Next came my mom's greeting. I worked in the nursery on Sunday mornings, so I typically arrived a little early to set up, then headed into the Great Room to listen to my mom and the worship band rehearse. When I walked into the Great Room that morning, my mom said excitedly into the microphone, "Happy Mother's Day!" What many people may have thought was an embarrassed reaction was really just me processing it. I hadn't ever been wished that before (other than from my dad), so I was honestly just asking myself, "How does a mother react?" I went with "thank you" and an awkward smile, but it meant the world to me. I knew it had to be strange for my mom as well, not only because of my situation, but also because now she'd be sharing the holiday that for the past 20 years had solely been her day. She and I have grown to be very good at sharing things (clothes, makeup, cars, etc.), so I knew we would be fine.

My first Mother's Day ended up being a total blessing. All the love and encouragement I received was unbelievable. I felt like I was being welcomed into the "Motherhood Club." At home, my brother had shipped two adorable bouquets of flowers, one for my mom and one for me. His thoughtfulness has always blown me away. The rest of the day, though, my focus was still very much about loving my own mother. I wanted her to feel appreciated, especially for all she had done for me during the previous six months. I was daily amazed by the sacrifices my parents continued to make to help me get through my situation. On Mother's Day, what better gift to have received than a perfect example and role model of the kind of mother I hoped to be in just a few more months.

Home Sweet Home

As expected, my last semester of college flew by at lightning speed. When I thought back on all that I had accomplished over the previous four years, I was incredibly thankful for my 3 F's: faith, family, and friends. Without them, I would never have made it this far. There were so many life-altering moments over the past four years when I turned to them to help guide me in the right direction. My college experience molded me into a new daughter in Christ. My faith grew considerably through all of my undesirable circumstances, as well as through fellowship with amazing friends. My family and friends stuck by me through all the good and the bad. I couldn't have asked for a better college experience.

A few months before graduation, I dreaded leaving the college life with all of my friends. There really was a carefree way about life in college. Generally, your biggest worry is what assignment is due next, or where you would find your next meal. However, I soon became eager to return to my parents' house and enjoy the comfort that goes with home life. I often joked with my parents about how much I missed my own bed (which is undeniably the most comfortable bed in the world). Getting a better night's sleep was just one of the many perks about being back home. I also felt safer knowing my parents were right down the hall. Some of my roommates' plans for emergency situations were pretty well thought out while others were more comical, and yet none felt as comforting as home.

Back at home, I started preparing for little peanut. It was important to me that she have a name before we prepared the nursery, because I had hoped to incorporate it somehow. After much debate among the names on our list, Mateo and I finally settled on the name Adrianna. My grandparents from Florida came into town for my graduation, and my "Pop-Pop" helped my dad and brother build the baby crib for me. Mom spent some time painting my room "apple green" to match the crib bedding, and we brought in the dresser and changing table that matched the crib. Very rapidly, my room became half nursery, half me. It was like a surprise party every morning when I woke up and looked across the room to see the beautiful crib. And yet, it made me incredibly nervous to think about how in about two months, there would be a baby in that crib.

At 29 weeks along, I looked bigger than ever. From my bird's eye view, my belly looked borderline obese. But from the side, I appeared to be most definitely pregnant. I was no longer embarrassed to wear tighter shirts in public. I felt weird when I knew my belly was showing on campus at school, but I didn't get that feeling in my hometown. I guess I felt like I blended in more. Most importantly, being home meant more time with family; more family meals, more family movies, more family talks, etc. Although moving back home to live with my parents may not have been my ideal, I'm found it to be good timing for that season of my life. Once Adrianna arrived, I would need that family time more than ever, and so would she.

Dreaming of Peanut

My family and roommates would be the first to tell you that I have some of the most extraordinarily detailed and bizarre dreams ever. So it was no surprise to me that these dreams became even stranger after becoming pregnant. By my third trimester, Adrianna played at least a small role in my dream world almost every night. In one of my recurring dreams, Adrianna was just a small infant, but was having an adult conversation with me. At first I just dismissed this as being one of my typical strange dreams. However, while reading my "What to Expect" book, I read that peculiar dreams come with the pregnancy package and that many of them can be meaningful. I thought for sure my dreams were oddball enough to not make it into the book, but lo and behold, there it was: my dream about baby Adrianna talking to me. Apparently, this kind of dream is common and stems from anxiety about not knowing how to care for an infant. That pretty much hit the nail on the head, because the closer I got to Adrianna's birth, the more I worried about it. Give me a two-year-old toddler or older, and I'm golden. It takes very little effort, for the most part, to keep them entertained (at least from what I've experienced while babysitting). But an infant? I worried about the long crying episodes. I could already picture myself frantically trying anything and everything to make her stop crying. Since she wouldn't be able to tell me what she wanted, who knew how long it would take for me to gain that incredible maternal skill of deciphering different cries?

The image I had in my mind was a little comical. I envisioned a very sleep-deprived version of myself with crazy, unwashed hair and mismatched clothes. I was holding Adrianna, who was screaming her little head off, while I was running around changing her diaper, feeding her, burping her, dancing with her . . . on and on and on. The more I sat and thought about it, the less funny it became. I was sure my parents were looking forward to having front row seats to such entertainment. After all, it was like payback for all the times I surely did the exact same thing.

Thinking of things like that quickly became overwhelming. I'll admit I often found myself thinking how hard this journey would be. I even started to occasionally watch that terrible show on TV called, "16 and Pregnant," to remind myself that my situation could be worse and to take note of things *not* to do throughout my pregnancy. It blew me away to see girls much younger than me approach the same situation with a mindset that everything would just fall into place without effort. It seemed they thought having a child would be a piece of cake. Without a doubt, I had faith that everything would work out according to God's will, which is ultimately the best outcome anyway. But without effort? Heck no! I knew that from the minute little Peanut was born, my effort to be a mom would never stop. From preparing bottles to fixing "boo-boo's" to comforting her through those terrible middle school gossip frenzies . . . I couldn't envision motherhood ever requiring anything *less* than significant effort. But that's coming from a girl whose mom is still putting in an insurmountable effort to be my mother.

Once I recognized my anxiety about being a mother to an infant, I was able to redirect my thoughts to some of the exciting parts of infancy that may help to balance out the difficulties. For example, I recently had the opportunity to spend five minutes or so holding a six-week-old baby girl. I had forgotten how adorable it is when a baby that small is able to crack a toothless smile! That first smile, the first laugh, the first yawn, the first coo . . . those are just some of the many blessings I knew God would use to encourage me to push forward through the difficulties of caring for an infant.

"You're Lucky"

I still got nervous when I talked to people about my pregnancy, and I didn't know why. I had yet to receive any sort of negative response, so I shouldn't really be fearful of that. For the most part, I got nervous about the unknown. I never knew how someone would react. My nervousness about the unknown while sharing the news with my closest friends and family was by far the most immense. Since then, it became easier to share, especially with complete strangers. I'm still working on completely ridding myself of the shame and guilt (thoughI am confident in God's unconditional love and forgiveness), but I think strangers were the easiest to tell because they were completely unaware of the story behind my pregnancy. For all they knew, I may have just left my wedding ring at home. Because of that, they were generally very optimistic about everything, so I rarely hesitated to share the news with them.

On one occasion, however, I had a completely unexpected response from a stranger. My mother and I were trying to figure out how to make my half of the room more mature, while creating a sweet little jungle theme for Adrianna. We went shopping to find some blinds that would block out the sunlight that always found its way right into my face every morning before my alarm had the chance to go off. We had already decided on the type of blinds at the store, but needed some help with the measurements and style. The lady working in the "window treatment" department helped us look through a huge book of different styles and textures. After a while, my mom mentioned that the blinds would be for a nursery and that they needed to block out light. The lady then asked me when I was due. My response sounded a bit rehearsed, due to the number of times I said it in recent weeks. I couldn't really describe the look she had on her face, but I knew what she was about to say would be different from what I was used to hearing.

The woman looked at me and my belly and said, "You're lucky." At first, I was very taken aback because I couldn't possibly understand why anyone would consider my situation a lucky one. In that instant, I assumed she had figured out by my interactions with my mother that I was young and unmarried. She then went on to explain, "I could stand on my head and try in-vitro and still not conceive." All the while, her sister had three children of her own.

The rest of our time in the store, I couldn't have cared less about what blinds we ordered. I had been looked at for months, and not once felt like it was out of envy. I couldn't wrap my mind around what the woman had said or how she could be envious of what I considered to be the toughest time of my life. Then I remembered a Bible verse I had stumbled upon earlier in my pregnancy: "Behold, children are a gift of the Lord. The fruit of the womb is a reward" (Psalm 127:3). I have known for a long time that some women are unable to conceive—not by any fault of their own, but out of God's divine plan for their lives, as difficult as it may be. In fact, I used to think about how devastating it would be one day to find out I couldn't conceive, considering how deeply passionate I am about children. But that was assuming I was farther down the road, married and prepared for starting a family.

What I had not considered was that my pregnancy even now and even this early is considered a reward and a divine privilege. For someone to tell me that I am "lucky" really was, to me, a reminder from God that despite the complicated timing, this pregnancy in His eyes was a reward. As humans, it is so easy to get wrapped up in the negatives and the tragedies of life and look past the blessings that come from them. This is not to say that I do not consider my daughter to be a blessing. I most certainly consider all babies a miracle of life and a blessing, but I have no doubt in my mind that God wanted me to feel and believe that Adrianna was not only a blessing, but a reward; a divine gift that some women may never experience. And for that I am truly thankful. For seven months, I had considered myself one of the unluckiest people I knew. Isn't it amazing the way God chooses to encourage His children when they need it?

Love Covers It All

"Above all, love each other deeply, because love covers a multitude of sins" (1 Peter 4:8). The meaning of this verse changed for me during the first seven months of my pregnancy. At first, it gave me the reassurance that my family and friends would be forgiving and loving in my darkest hour. Now it means all of that and more. It is interesting to me that this verse doesn't apply to Christians only. I experienced incredible love from family and friends, some of whom would not consider themselves to be believers. I knew that some people would be accepting of me and offer kind gestures of encouragement, but I never expected to receive compassion and love.

One example occurred when some of my mother's friends from church got together and planned a baby shower for me. I couldn't comprehend why women who barely knew me would want to put in the time and effort required to plan and throw a baby shower. I learned from the baby shower my roommates gave me that it's hard work! Just as with my first baby shower, I was slightly anxious about what the experience would be like. I can't really explain what it feels like to have a party that celebrates an unplanned pregnancy, other than to say that I definitely felt undeserving. However, within just moments of being there, I was reminded of what the party was truly celebrating: the miracle of life.

The women welcomed my mother and me with loving smiles and excitement. It was obvious they had spent quite a bit of time preparing everything. I spent a lot of time talking to each of the women and enjoying the time with them. I also spent some time observing the women talk amongst themselves. It made me feel very special that they were gathered there joyfully celebrating my soon-to-be-born daughter.

The women also gave some incredibly thoughtful gifts! I could write pages about each gift and its meaning to me. The women were very intentional about showing me their love and compassion, not only for my daughter, but for me as well. God has been so faithful in reminding me that I am loved by others because He first loved me.

This domino effect of love gave me a greater understanding of the love I feel for my daughter. I had been struggling with not knowing how or when my motherly love would set in. I would see other expectant moms just gleaming with the love they already felt for their child. It wasn't that I didn't want Adrianna or love her already. I most definitely loved her, even in my very first shock of her existence. I was just waiting for that undeniably unconditional mother-child love that only a mother can describe. I realized after the baby shower that each time there was a moment of excitement for her arrival, I fall even more in love with her. The excitement factor pulls me forward into the reality and the joy of a new life. There have been several exciting moments along the way, including baby showers, baby purchases, making her crib, etc. I just hadn't realized how each of those moments grew me to become even more excited about her arrival and even more ready to love her as unconditionally as so many people have loved me.

Stork Parking

I definitely did not consider myself to be one of the lucky ladies who experiences that "pregnancy glow" with longer, thicker nails, luscious locks of hair, and smooth, flawless skin. In fact, my body decided to react in the most opposite way possible. My nails became brittle and broke without reason. My hair (although longer) had a mind of its own and could not be tamed by the strongest of hairsprays. My skin seemed to find some way to irritate me from day to day. I was disappointed by my lack of the "glow" because I had considered it to be one of the only perks of being pregnant.

However, I did discover an unexpected perk called stork parking! The only places I have been that had this magnificent feature were the toy store and the grocery store. But since I seemed to go to both of those places frequently, I thoroughly enjoyed what I considered to be a V.I.P. parking spot.In the past, I considered my trips to the grocery store to be a success if I could leave without having become frustrated by the lack of parking spaces, those slow walking aisle-hogs, or the food items that were inexplicably placed on an aisle that made no sense at all. Peanut butter and jelly is now at the end of the ice cream aisle . . . *what?* At least parking would not be an issue for the next few months.

God knows I am not the most patient person and I often joked about how He designates certain days to test me. Late in my pregnancy, these days seemed to occur much more frequently. I had no doubt God was preparing me for motherhood. I knew that taking care of an infant was especially difficult with regard to patience, since babies are incapable of expressing their wants and needs. God used little things to prepare me. Although frustrating at the time, the chain of events that seemed intentionally planned to test my patience were quite humorous. For example, one day I was rushing to print off an important document before leaving to run errands. However, it was as if everything was working against me to prevent the document from printing. Several attempts on my mom's ancient laptop only led to frustration. I then moved to my dad's computer, which was working at its absolute slowest, just to spite me, I'm sure. As I finally got the document to print, it somehow jammed three sheets of paper through at the same time, making my document a scattered mess. In my increasing frustration, I angrily tried to print it again, only to discover the printer was out of paper!

I believe God used my pregnancy to help grow me in numerous ways. Besides the obvious physical growth, He used my pregnancy to grow me emotionally and spiritually, as well. Being pregnant forced me to evaluate myself and prepare to become the best mom I can be. My patience is just one of the spiritual fruits this pregnancy taught me to work on, and I have undoubtedly learned some important life lessons. Thankfully, when it comes to parking, God gives me a little break.

Bringing the Hidden into the Light

> "*So do not be afraid of them, for there is nothing concealed that will not be disclosed, or hidden that will not be made known.*" – Matthew 10:26

Any girl will tell you that there is no such thing as a secret. Although we share them consistently with the false hope of complete confidentiality, we all know that the majority of the time the secret only stays secret for so long. The smaller, seemingly insignificant secrets are sometimes easier to keep, only because they are quickly forgotten. But when the more intriguing, gossip-sparking secrets are shared, generally those secrets are public knowledge just as soon as they are told, especially today with social interaction at our fingertips. One touch of a button can send a text to anyone and everyone who may care (or not care) to know the latest gossip. Because of this common understanding that no secret is kept, our human tendency is to conceal our personal secrets, flaws, and failures, and reveal them to no one. Revealing such secrets, after all, can make us vulnerable to public criticism and judgment. But this way of thinking is so backwards!

I never really made the conscious decision *not* to hide my pregnancy. I recognized from the very beginning that it would only be easily hidden for a short amount of time, so there seemed to be no reason for hiding it at all. Keeping anything from my parents is a challenge itself, mainly because we have such a close relationship. If I so much as breathe a different way, they somehow instantly know there is something going on—a skill I hope to gain as a mom. So hiding my pregnancy from my parents never even crossed my mind.

In the beginning, I was very intentional about who I shared the news with. I wanted to be in control of my secret until I was able to tell everyone I would want to personally share it with. Yet, within only a few weeks, the news had spread like wildfire. At first, I was pretty angry. Although I knew that my secret was definitely too big to keep for very long, I had a hard time swallowing the fact that people were so comfortable sharing it for their own enjoyment. But once I re-evaluated it all, I realized that if I had discovered the same news about someone else, it would probably have been pretty hard for me not to share it in a weak moment, too.

As time went on and my belly grew bigger, I had the choice to either conceal my bump or not. The days I chose to wear baggier clothes and hide my bump were the days I felt the most self-conscious. After spending a day at the lake, talking to some of the most awesome women you would ever meet, I came to realize the reasons for my self-consciousness when I was "in hiding." Those days were the days I could feel Satan forcing negativity into my mind. I could feel him bringing me down, finding any and every insecurity I was feeling and using it to destroy my confidence. However, the days I was a little bolder and threw on the tight maternity shirts were the days I felt the most confident in God's plan for my pregnancy and life.

After some thought and conversation with the women at the lake, I realized my confidence to share my "secret" came from an understanding of the peace that comes with bringing the hidden into the light. Concealing a personal secret can be hard work. It often requires you to come up with cover stories and lies, which always cause situations to be considerably uncomfortable. On the other hand, revealing a personal secret brings relief. Sharing a secret is scary, no doubt, because you never know who will use it against you. But I can tell you from this experience that the majority of the time, it is surprising how many doors it will open and people it can reach in unexpected ways.

Having said this, I was in no way broadcasting my pregnancy or shouting it from rooftops. I typically waited for the question, "What are you doing after you graduate?" I considered this to be God's way of giving me a little nudge. Sharing my secret got easier over time, especially since every time I shared it, God gave me another person to encourage and support me. That's not to say that revealing my secret was easy or brought only positivity. There were, of course, the few occasions in which I was clearly being judged or criticized. But by then, I had gained such an abundance of people supporting me that the negativity only fazed me for a short time.

I think all of this can relate back to that "child-like faith" I wrote about earlier. Children may have a more simplified view of life, but I consider it to be the best view sometimes. Many children have an understanding early on that "evil things" reside in the darkness. Obviously, this relates more to physical darkness and the mythical monster living in the closet. But in relation to keeping personal secrets, children have it right! As long as it is in the dark, it only brings about fear, anxiety, and self-consciousness. Just as any parent would tell you, the remedy is to turn on the light!

Guess that Bump

As I continued to get bigger, Adrianna's space quickly got smaller. There wasn't enough room for fiesta parties anymore. Strong and vigorous dance moves turned into slow yoga stretches. I imagine we were probably all our most flexible at birth, after having spent several months as a contortionist inside the womb. Because of her slower, more drastic moves, I was able to see her little stretches through the skin on my belly. Feeling the little bump makes it more obvious that it's her. It is clearly a hard, round something. Mom and I enjoyed lying in bed waiting for her little stretches as I read to her at night. I think she started to recognize "Buenas Noches Luna" and "Eres Mi Mama?" because it didn't take long for her to start wiggling around when I read them. As she moved here and there, we could feel distinct, hard bumps beneath my skin. We enjoyed playing "Guess that Bump" by trying to figure out which body part she was using to prod me.

One night, as Mom and I laid in bed waiting for Adrianna's late night debut, she finally started wiggling around. Just as I did the very first time, I still got a giggle out of feeling her move around. But as I started to laugh, I looked at my stomach. What had been a round basketball-like belly suddenly turned cone-shaped. Due to my laughter and the way my abs were contracting, my stomach literally took on the form of a cone with the point being right at my bellybutton. This only set my mom and I off in a laughing frenzy. Of course, each time I laughed, the cone came back and only egged us on more.

Once the laughter calmed and my mom left for bed, I thought back on that moment and realized that it had been an incredibly long time since I had laughed so hard. I enjoy humor, *a lot*, and anyone who knows my father and brother would agree that living with them is like living in a constant stand-up comedy routine. Humor has a comforting feel to me and I've been known to use it in uncomfortable situations, either to ease the tension or take the attention off of the issue at hand. But despite the constant flow of humor in my life, I hadn't really felt true, physical joy in the form of deep, uncontrollable laughter in quite some time.

I had allowed myself to view my situation as being humorless. The reality of an unplanned pregnancy is anything but funny. I had been able to laugh at some of the petty jokes and things, but when I sat and considered all that my pregnancy and future as a mother entailed, humor escaped me. All the worries of becoming a mom consumed me . . . until that moment in bed. That was the first time I could look at myself and really laugh at the idea that my daughter was growing inside me and would soon be in the world.

It was a great reminder of what my counselor at the crisis pregnancy center told me and what I had then passed on to my parents the night after sharing the news with them. She said, "God never gives you anything that you can't handle." That idea had been pushed to the back of my mind, but in my fit of laughter, I recognized how far God had carried me. To be able to laugh like that, for me, was a sign that God and I had handled a lot. It was a laughter of joy and relief. I'd made it through what I considered to be the toughest part so far, all because God knew I could handle it.

Babies Have FINGERNAILS!

My freshman year of college seemed like only yesterday, along with all of its amusing memories. The Virginia Tech campus is a big one, but after spending four years there, the majority of places on campus had memories attached. Most of those memories came from time spent with friends in the dorm. I was blessed to live on a hallway of Christian girls who had agreed to sign a contract stating they would not drink or smoke while living there. While most students were enjoying the college party life, we found ways to entertain ourselves on campus or in the dorm. When there wasn't a new game to play or an on-campus event to attend, we watched movies, several of which we enjoyed so much that we watched multiple times. The movie I most distinctly remember watching over and over again was *Juno*. It's a comedy about a quirky girl in high school who finds out that she is pregnant. Her attitude about the whole situation is incredibly humorous, all while she tries to make the best decisions for her baby.

My mom and I watched it again after my graduation, for the first time since my freshman year. I could appreciate so much more about the movie, having dealt with an unplanned pregnancy myself. Some of Juno's witty comments were much more comical to me. In the beginning of the movie, after she discovers she is pregnant, Juno seeks help at a local abortion clinic. As she enters the clinic, one of her classmates is picketing outside and makes several attempts to change Juno's mind. In a last attempt to stop Juno, the girl states, "Babies have fingernails." Juno is surprised by the comment and ends up leaving the clinic with the intention to continue the pregnancy and give the baby to adoptive parents. When another friend later confronts Juno on her decision against abortion, her explanation ends with an exasperated, ". . . and babies have fingernails . . . FINGERNAILS!" Although true, this fact really had no effect on my decision to have my baby. Juno's revelation about the baby having fingernails, although comical, is so relevant because it's the simple facts like fingernails that change the minds of many girls going through the same situation. For me, these statements are now just affirmations that I made a good decision.

Each week, I love reading in my "What to Expect" book about the amazing ways my daughter is growing. From Day One, I've enjoyed reading about her newest feature like the hardening of her bones, her ability to move, her growing brain, her ability to hear my voice, and her ability to have dreams. Each time I read something new, I am just as amazed as the first time. I know her development does not stop once she is born and it's scary to think about how she will no longer be in the safety of my womb to do all of that growing. But I know that with each new step in her future growth, I will continue to be just as amazed as Juno was. And since my baby is a girl, I can look forward to painting those little fingernails!

Bigfoot Birthday

Just as I do every summer, I completely lost track of the days. I often had to remind myself what day of the week it was, and my "gestational Alzheimer's" (as I began to call it) really didn't help the situation. I'd never been so forgetful before and it became pretty frustrating not to remember what day it was or what I was supposed to be doing. If Adrianna was "sucking up all my brain cells" like so many people described, by that time I supposed she would come out talking!

Thanks to my absentmindedness, it wasn't until four days before my birthday, which is in the middle of the month, that I realized we were even in my birth month. Over the years I've come to recognize that each birthday becomes less and less exciting, unless of course it's a special one like 18 or 21. I was somewhat excited about turning 22 that year because it made me less young, and therefore not as young of a mom. But I came to the realization that the whole idea of a birthday had lost its sparkle.

I realized that, just as Adrianna was sucking all of my brain cells, she was also sucking all of my excitement. It was hard to be excited about my own birthday when hers was getting so close. Nonetheless, my family and friends made my day incredibly fun and special. We have a family tradition of serving breakfast in bed to the birthday boy or girl, so I was served delicious pancakes and fresh strawberries in my bed. Mom surprised me and bought the finishing touches for my half nursery/half adult bedroom. Since Adrianna's crib theme is "Jungle Jill" with lots of cute, brightly-colored jungle animals and prints, Mom and I decided the best way to match and keep my half of the room mature would be to go with an adult jungle theme. I now had a giraffe print comforter and sheets with cute, decorative pillows!

My birthday was busy, just as most days were after I completely overfilled my schedule in fear of not having anything to do during the summer. Most of what I did could be done sitting down, but just going from one thing to the next wore me out. One unpleasant addition to my busy, exhausting days was the spontaneous and unpredictable swelling of my feet. Standing up, sitting down, laying down . . . it didn't matter. As soon as I felt them start to swell, I knew I had about one minute to remove my shoes or I'd have to cut them off.

My mom, being as awesome as she is, offered her foot-massaging services to me every night, which was nothing less than heavenly. It really was amazing to me how quickly my feet could look like balloons, which was most certainly not an attractive feature. Of course, the random swelling came at the most inopportune times, such as the moment all my friends arrived to celebrate my birthday. I removed my cute sandals and, we'll just say, celebrated barefoot in honor of Bigfoot.

I got into the bad habit of complaining about some of the silly side effects of pregnancy without taking much time to consider how God might be using them to my benefit. I knew He must have had a reason, but making me more absentminded and giving me unnaturally huge feet hardly seemed like ways to prepare me for motherhood. I knew I was going to need all the brain cells I could get to be able to function through all the sleep-deprived thought processes early on, like scheduling appointments and deciphering baby cries. Having swollen feet would only add to my frustrations.

But it's possible that these were just a few of God's little reminders that I really had no control. As much as I wanted to have it all together, I still walked upstairs and couldn't remember why. And no matter what I did with my feet to prevent the swelling, they inevitably continued to balloon like never before. Through it all, I could surely rely on my confidence that God was in control and He would get me through it. After all, He has gotten me through much harder times. With that reminder, I guess I should have been thankful for my absent mind and my big ol' feet.

"A Brook Would Lose its Song if God Removed the Rocks"

There's a church not too far from my house that I passed pretty frequently on my way to town. I have memories of anxiously waiting in my pajamas in a long line of cars to drive through the "Live Nativity Scene" the church had every year at Christmas. I used to watch in amazement as we drove through the different scenes of Jesus' birth with real people and animals and angels singing from their posts high up on the church wall. They even had a real baby in the manger playing the role of baby Jesus. The nativity scene is gone just as soon as it arrives and for the other 11 months of the year, the church appears empty except on Sundays. However, every couple of weeks, someone at the church puts a new, intriguing phrase on the sign by the road.

I have driven by that church hundreds of times. I can recall many instances in which I admired the new quote or phrase, but didn't put much thought into it. That was until one occasion when God might as well have smacked me across the head with it. The sign read, "A brook would lose its song if God removed the rocks."

Over the next few days as I passed by that sign on my way into town, I was amazed by how God kept putting the quote on my mind as a quiet reminder. I thought about how many of my prayers consisted of me asking God to remove the challenges, or "rocks" I faced in my day-to-day life. I so often looked at my "rocks" with frustration and anger. After all, who actually wants to have a rocky life? I can't ever recall praying, "Dear Lord, please give me more challenges. My life just isn't challenging enough." But I can so easily look back on my life so far and see how intricately God placed the rocks in my path to help me grow and get to where I am.

So why am I so quick to become frustrated by the new challenges God puts before me? Being pregnant was no easy process. I could have built a pretty big wall around myself with all the rocks God gave me. That would have been the easy thing to do; just ignore the rocks, give up, and let them add up around me infinitely. Instead, God has been incredibly faithful at giving me the strength to move swiftly and confidently past the rocks, just as the water in a brook. Although painful and difficult at times, I somehow made it around even the biggest of the rocks, and even though there are certainly more rocks to come, soon I'll have a cute and cuddly baby girl who is sure to reflect the beautiful song created by the rocks God so intricately placed in my brook.

Hiccups

From the time I started being able to feel Adrianna kick, I had been waiting for her first case of the hiccups. I had read in my "What to Expect" book about the rhythmic movement I would feel that would be different from her typical kicks and tumbles. The book also reassured me that for babies in the womb, hiccups are no big deal. Hiccups can be irritating for adults, so I'm sure it's not uncommon for a mother to be a little concerned at first when her little one starts hiccupping uncontrollably, especially if they start like Adrianna's did. I had gotten used to her having late night fiesta dance parties as I tried to fall asleep, so feeling her movement was no surprise. But after a few moments, I realized it was not at all like her typical dance moves. I could feel and see her little jump very consistently for about five minutes. I envy God for His ability to see Adrianna at all times because I would have loved to see her in that moment, having her first case of the hiccups.

Since then, she got the hiccups almost every day. Sometimes they were fast and short-lived, other times they were very slow and could last up to 20 minutes. Either way, I loved being able to feel her move, knowing she was still doing alright in there. Each time she had the hiccups, I was reminded of one of my favorite childhood comics: Calvin & Hobbes. My brother and I used to read them together, and I have memories of laughing with him until I cried. Calvin is a small, rebellious boy with an incredible imagination. The cartoons typically consisted of his funny adventures with his stuffed Tiger, Hobbes. This is one of my favorites:

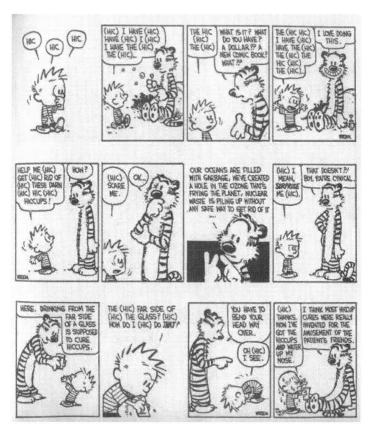

God is Not Surprised

This pregnancy has been a surprise from the beginning. Obviously, an unplanned pregnancy comes as a bit of a shock to everyone. Aside from the initial surprise, there are many more surprises that come along with being pregnant. The first ultrasound and getting to hear the heartbeat, the first time she kicked and wiggled, when I found out she was a girl, and the many times God surprised me with special people to encourage me along the way. The list could go on and on, but the point is that surprises are to be expected in a pregnancy, unplanned or not.

From the beginning, as I think most mothers experience, there's this innate desire to prepare for the baby. At first, when you can't even tell the baby is there, it's hard to really grasp all that is going on within. And yet, there is still such an excitement and anxiety about eating the right foods, avoiding the pregnancy "no-no's," or buying the right baby stuff. Luckily, I was incredibly blessed to have an amazing support system of friends and women in my life who cared for me through love, prayers, and baby gifts.

At 34 weeks, I had another amazing baby shower! The room was filled with women who have continually been an incredible support for me, directly and indirectly. They all joyfully showered me with love and beautiful gifts and a beautifully special prayer. As excited as I was about this much anticipated party, I was still so surprised by the amount of love I felt from everyone there.

Aside from gorgeous gifts, the women also took the time to write down tidbits of advice for me on little pink and brown cards. They had awesome words of motherly wisdom that I am sure to use throughout Adrianna's life. As the time drew closer to her arrival, I became much more focused on the many aspects of parenting and much less focused on the actual pregnancy.

At my 35-week appointment, I was humbled by experiencing the first unpleasant surprise of my pregnancy. The doctor's visit started out just like all the others. First, the long wait in the waiting room. Luckily I had my mom and dad there with me this time to keep me entertained. If you knew my father, you would know that he is serious about 2% of the time. My doctor's incredibly efficient nurse finally called us back to the examination room where she once again forced me onto the scale. She always acted so nice about how much weight I gained, but I was sure that's just part of her job because I saw the same numbers she did and they made me want to scream!

Once the doctor came in, she proceeded to do the normal check-up, like listening to the heartbeat and palpating my huge belly. After measuring my stomach, however, she explained that little Adrianna seemed to be on the smaller side of average, so she wanted to perform an ultrasound to measure and get look at her. I was thrilled because ultrasounds were few and far between during pregnancy, and I was anxious to see her again. But, just as with the 20-week ultrasound, the little diva wouldn't show her face as she moved around on camera. We watched as the ultrasound technician measured the back of her head, her stomach, and her arms, legs, and feet. The ultrasound, although a good 15 minutes long, flew by so it wasn't much longer before we were back in the examination room to hear about the measurements.

My excitement quickly turned to panic as the doctor explained that Adrianna was not only faced the wrong way for birth ("breech"), but she also appeared to have a small abdomen size proportionally to her head. Generally, this is an indication that she had "growth restriction" due to a problem with the placenta. Calmly, the doctor explained that there was a good chance the measurements may have been off, thanks to all of her squirming around. She also recommended that I come in two times a week to monitor the condition.

Although the doctor seemed optimistic about it all, my mind still focused only on the negative that I had heard. I tried to smile confidently as she told me the news, but I broke down soon after leaving the office. I can't really explain my emotions in that moment other than to say that I was scared and angry. I was scared of all of those percentages and numbers in reference to the worst-case scenarios and where Adrianna might fall. For a short while, I was angry at God for throwing such a terrifying surprise at me so close to the delivery.

I spent the rest of the day considering all that I had been told and thinking through all the possible outcomes. I think God sensed my feeling of helplessness and shock because He also had divinely planned for my mom and I to have a dinner date with two of our close, encouraging friends. We spent a lot of the dinner talking about my appointment and Adrianna. Toward the end of the dinner, one of the women shared some encouraging words with me that made me think about it all in a totally different way. She said, "God is NOT surprised."

Up until that moment, in my shock and anger, I had only thought about how I felt. I was so surprised about the news that I had not once considered the fact that God was not surprised at all! I have talked about and heard about "God's plan" frequently, but in my moment of shock, it had completely slipped my mind. Just as this pregnancy and all of its surprises have been part of His plan from Day One, so was this appointment and the surprise that came with it.

I'm so thankful that God isn't surprised by the big and small "crises" we face in life. There is definitely a comfort that comes with knowing that He knew it all along. Everything would be a whole lot more terrifying if God was up there saying, "Oh wow, I didn't see that coming," especially with a new life and the many different complications that can arise during pregnancy. The fact that God was up there, nodding His head in agreement with the doctor's message, made me all the more reassured that He also knew and was in control of the outcome. Since He was NOT surprised, I could rest, praying and knowing that He still held my daughter in His hands. From beginning to end, every single day of her creation was no surprise to Him. Therefore, neither was this news.". . . Surely, as I have planned, so it will be, and as I have purposed, so it will happen" (Isaiah 12:24).

Good Things Come in Small Packages

Children treasure any holiday when gifts are given. I think adults enjoy them just as much, but as adults, we're older and more humble and don't want to be overly excited about others spending money for our enjoyment. As I've gotten older, one thing that's different for sure is that now I can actually sleep the night before my birthday and Christmas. I remember laying wide awake for hours as a child, just begging for the time to go faster. Being a June baby, my "gift-giving holidays" were pretty spread out. By Christmas, I had been thinking for six months about the latest, greatest thing I wanted to ask for. My parents often joked that they wished my brother and I had watched more TV so that we would have asked for normal, more easy-to-find gifts. Instead, we had all of our imagination to help us come up with the perfect gift list. My brother was a lot more imaginative than I was. One Christmas story that gets told over and over in our family is the Christmas he asked for an "elephant piggy bank." Rather than throwing up their arms, admitting defeat and revealing the secret behind Santa, my parents actually found a woman who made elephant piggy banks!

No matter what holiday it was or what crazy gift ideas we had come up with, I remember my brother and I marveling at the presents that appeared so much larger than the rest. Anxiously, we would wait to see what was inside the biggest box. Now, at 22 years of age, the gifts I remember the most, and the gifts with the most meaning, certainly didn't come in the biggest box. In fact, my parents would often chuckle at what I'm sure was a disappointed face as I was given a small box to open. The reason I think I must have looked disappointed to them was because they would always say, "Lauren . . . sometimes BIG things come in small boxes." And somehow, they were always right. Small boxes always had the meaningful gifts inside. I'm sure my life-size Barbie came in a pretty big box, but I barely remember opening that gift like I remember opening the sentimental pieces of jewelry, or the Precious Moments collectibles, or the plane tickets to Florida . . . the list goes on and on.

All this to say that I grew up with an appreciation for the smaller gifts in life. They always had a bigger impact on me. And so, it was no surprise to me that what will definitely be the most precious gift I've ever received is coming to me in a "smaller than average" package. At my next doctor's appointment, they began monitoring Adrianna's stress level and heartbeat to make sure she didn't have the "growth restriction" they had talked about before. After sitting for 30 minutes in a chair with belts strapped to me, the doctor informed me that Adrianna's responses were normal and that she was most likely just a "smaller than average" baby. HALLELUJAH! I praised God not only for the news that her health was fine, but also that I wouldn't be having one of those record-size babies you see on television, like 22 pounds? Those women deserve an award!

I sat there listening to the doctor explain that small measurements are typically just that . . . small measurements for a small baby. All I could think about was how grateful I was for her little life. I'm sure God was disappointed to see me instantly fear the worst when He knew the reality of her small size. He calls us to trust Him in all situations, good and bad, and although at some point I was able to let it go and give it up to Him, I had instantly settled in fear and anger. Sometimes, however, it takes situations like that to wake us up from our comfortable state, shake us a little, and remind us that we are not in control. I would have given anything to be able to help Adrianna in that moment, but thank goodness I didn't have that capability, because only God knew she didn't need help. He wanted to surprise me with the greatest gift of all, in a small, divinely created package. And with that, instantly all of my child-like excitement came flooding back, because oh, how I couldn't wait to open it!

The Home Stretch

I finally arrived at the "home stretch." At 36 weeks, most pregnancy books and physicians would consider me to be "full term," meaning that in the unlikely event that Adrianna would want to make her debut appearance the next day, they would allow her to do so without much concern. Although the chances of her arriving early were low, Adrianna continued to enjoy keeping me on my toes. After the "growth restriction" scare, I felt as if I'd been on 24-hour alertmode. Anything out of the ordinary made me nervous, as I suspect most moms felt at that point in their pregnancy. Luckily, my doctor and her nurse were incredibly understanding of the hyper-anxiety syndrome a lot of pregnant women must experience, because they responded fairly quickly to my weekly nervous phone calls.

My twice-a-week appointments became an absolute blessing and gave me a much greater peace of mind. Week 36, however, turned into an epic week of ultrasounds. After a little scare on that Thursday morning, my doctor asked me to come in for my second of three ultrasounds for the week. Although I had some concerns about Adrianna's health, I was excited for the chance to see her face on the ultrasound screen. By that point I'd had five ultrasounds, each with a brief period at the end when the ultrasound tech searched for a good angle to view Adrianna's face in 3D. And each time, Adrianna decided at the last minute to do a little dance that almost always resulted in her face being hidden. In fact, during one of the ultrasounds, she managed to turn her head almost completely around to face my back, something the ultrasound tech said she had never seen before.

During Thursday's ultrasound, Adrianna kept her hands over her face the whole time and somehow managed to put her fist in her mouth. So even though I got a very small glimpse of her eyes, the rest of her face appeared distorted. Although it was a bit disappointing that I had yet to get a glimpse of my daughter's face, it came as no surprise to me. At every single one of my doctor's visits, at least one person pointed out Adrianna's high activity level. "She's a mover!" and "You're gonna be chasing this one around!" were just a couple of the comments I heard. Not to mention, her breech position made it even more complicated to get a facial view.

Adrianna already showed signs of being a mini-me. Between being so active and busy and causing me almost constant anxiety, I had no doubt those were just a few of the things she and I would have in common. My parents remember me as a busy little girl, too—always getting into something, never slowing down. I'm pretty sure 90% of the grey hair on my father's head is due to something I did to worry him. I recently heard a song on the radio about a man who finds out he is having a son. Several times in the song he says, "heaven help him if he is anything like me." As I listened to it, it dawned on me that the moments my mom or dad said, "You'll understand when you have kids of your own" would soon become reality. If Adrianna was the little busy body that I was, I was sure my parents would enjoy every minute watching me try to handle those moments as beautifully as they did.

It quickly became more and more clear to me that Adrianna was the one in control of the rest of my pregnancy. Whereas the cheaper, more expected route of delivery would be natural birth, she conveniently positioned herself to be breech, making it necessary for a C-section. At first, this was a little upsetting for me because it wasn't at all how I had pictured the birth to take place. I envisioned the rush to the hospital, the long hours of contractions, and the long-awaited moment when she was delivered and placed in my arms. But it was as if Adrianna decided, "Eh . . . no. I'd rather come out the more expensive way with the more aesthetically pleasing head shape."

I adapted my mental plans to instead envision being wheeled into an operating room on a table and listening from behind a curtain as they essentially cut her out of m—and then a long recovery period before I could hold her in my arms for the first time. However, most of those negative thoughts left me on the Friday morning when my doctor announced, "Okay, let's get you on the schedule for the C-section." At first, it just seemed normal. Every appointment ended with a scheduling of the next appointment. But then it hit me: Did she just ask me to pick my daughter's birthday? I thought picking the name was a lot of pressure, but picking the birthday definitely surpassed that. Luckily, there was only one day in my 39th week that my doctor was on call. So, July 29th it was! Of course, that assumed Adrianna didn't continue with her trend of surprises and decide to show up sooner, which would not have surprised me in the least. After all, from day one, she has *loved* the element of surprise!

My Reality

The first thing I saw whenever I woke up each morning was Adrianna's crib. Above the crib hung her "Jungle Jill" blanket adorned with cute little jungle animals and animal patterns. As I walked out of my room, I passed her dresser filled with onesies, diapers, wipes, and swaddle blankets. Her changing pad, with a pink cover of course, laid on top of the dresser next to a basket full of diapers and an unopened tube of "Butt Paste." On the wall, there were some small round mirrors surrounding the wall art that matched her crib. My closet that once held all of my clothes, my way-too-many-pairs of shoes, and the random "junk" I just couldn't get rid of, was full of newborn outfits, lacy dresses, booties, pacifiers, baby hats, bows, wipes, diapers . . . you name it. A rocking chair sat by my bed with a side table covered in the Spanish versions of my favorite childhood books. In my bathroom closet, where all my lotions, bubble baths, hair supplies, and makeup used to be, there were now baby washcloths, towels, and enough Johnson & Johnson lotions and soaps to last an entire year.

In the living room, where my mom used to have decorative tables covered in some old family photos and potpourri, there was now a Pack n' Play, a bright pink Exersaucer and a baby swing that could practically do everything but change a diaper. One of the kitchen cabinets where the coffee supplies and mugs used to be now held baby bottles, pacifiers, spoons, drying racks, and bibs. The rearview vision in my car was a little smaller, with a baby mirror that reflected the image of an empty car seat in the back of my car, not to mention, my blind spot was a little harder to see with a baby sun shade screen that covered the whole window.

Needless to say, everything around me reflected the baby that would soon become my entire world. From the time I woke up to the time I went to sleep, my day was full of reminders in addition to my growing belly. It was very rare to have moments when being pregnant and Adrianna were not on my mind. When I envisioned the upcoming weeks, months, and even years, wherever I was, there was a little girl in my stroller or on my hip or walking alongside me. I pictured my life to be a lot messier, with a constant smell of baby powder or baby shampoo or worse, a dirty diaper. I pictured sleepless nights, wishing my efforts would soothe her enough to sleep for just another hour. Then I pictured the nights I would be wishing she were still small enough to rock to sleep. I pictured frantic meal times, food in my hair and hers, and laughing until my stomach hurt when she curiously licked a lemon for the first time.

All of these dreams and expectations for the future so perfectly replaced what I used to dream and think about. In fact, it had been so long since I considered my life *without* Adrianna that my life *with* her was all that I could imagine. It became easy to see that the things I had been hoping to do, the things that would be impossible with a child, were things that would not have been nearly as perfect for this time in my life as Adrianna will be. Although terrifying and devastating at first, my unplanned pregnancy and future as Adrianna's mother became much more real over time. Nine months earlier, I would never have been able to imagine myself at that stage in my pregnancy. But nine months later, I couldn't imagine myself anywhere else. Come July 29th, I was sure that feeling would only become stronger. Holding Adrianna for the first time would only amplify what had so quickly become my reality.

This is the Day that the Lord has Made

And I am soooo rejoicing and soooo glad in it! (Psalm 118:24). I had a hunch that July 21st, 2010 would play out the way it did, so for once my maternal instincts did not fail me. And what great timing! As the ultrasound technician checked my fluid levels, she very nonchalantly made the comment, "I'll try and get that baby here today." As exciting as that was, I was still skeptical and anxiously awaiting the doctor to see what she would recommend. Before I knew it, she was explaining to me, my mother, and Mateo how to get to the hospital and how to sign in. I'm sure we all had the same shocked, blank stare on our faces.

As we made the short drive over to the hospital, I had a rush of emotions—mainly excitement, but also an overwhelming feeling of, "Oh no, here we go." As of the previous day, I still had a full week to mentally prepare for what was suddenly approaching very rapidly. Instead, I had at most 24 hours. As weird as it sounds, all of a sudden it hit me how incredibly crazy it was that a small life was about to emerge from my tummy—a small life that would change mine forever.

With emotions still spinning wildly in my mind, we were escorted to the labor and delivery floor, where I was strapped to a fetal monitor. My anxiousness caused me to be pretty hyper for the first hour of monitoring. I knew that if Adrianna showed signs of distress, the doctor would prefer to move ahead with the C-section immediately. So, although I was anxious for her to arrive, I was relieved to hear that she was perfectly fine.

The doctor explained that they would bring her into the world at 12:30pm the next day. Not long after hearing that news, a pastor and a dear friend of mine came to visit and pray over Adrianna and me. Soon after they left, my dad and brother arrived with dinner. I'm not sure why, but seeing my younger brother was when it really hit me how quickly the past nine months had flown by. It seemed like just yesterday that I was sitting in his apartment sharing the news with him. He had been quick to remind me almost weekly since then that he expected to be the first person I called when Adrianna decided to make her debut. And now, nine months later, there we were, sitting in the hospital, all in a daze of amazement and nervousness.

After my brother and dad left, Mateo's family came to join in the excitement, and after them, two more dear friends of mine came to shower us in prayer once again. One thing was for sure: Adrianna and I made it through the pregnancy together thanks to the Lord and the power of prayer. The birth would be no different. As it was approaching so quickly, I realized it was not the big needles or intense surgery that I was most nervous about, but the beginning of my life as a mother. What a huge and divine responsibility! Just as God knew of Adrianna's existence before any of us could ever have imagined, He most certainly knew all the details of her arrival and beyond. I was confident that through Him and many more prayers, I would do my best to be the mother He must think I was able to be.

On July 22, 2011, I lay in a hospital bed at the very beginning of what was sure to be the best day of my life: the day my daughter, Adrianna, and I would meet for the first time. I knew that not having her in the comfort of my womb would take time to get used to, and I was sure I would miss the nightly blessing of feeling her kick, but for the moment I focused on the incredible blessing of that special day—a day God had known about all along, a day He had spent a great deal of time preparing her and me for, a day to rejoice and be glad in.

A Mother's Love

The range of emotions I felt before, during, and after the birth of my child was indescribable. In the hours leading up to meeting Adrianna, I was unexpectedly calm and full of excitement. It seemed that of everyone around me, I was the only one who had it together. After a full night of practically no sleep, all I could think about was the time and how quickly 12:30pm was approaching. Every time the door to my hospital room opened, I hoped it was a doctor coming in to escort me to the operating room.

Nurse after nurse came into my room to "check my vitals," a phrase I heard well over 100 times, and pump me with IV fluid. When 12:30 finally came, I tearfully walked down the hall to the O.R. with Mateo, leaving everyone else anxiously awaiting us in the waiting room. My nerves really didn't hit me until I was led alone into the O.R. for the pre-surgery prep. I tried to breathe calmly as I looked around the room at all of the intimidating equipment and the masked people wearing scrubs. The anesthesiologist proceeded to give me a spinal shot that numbed me from the chest down, which was undoubtedly the weirdest feeling I have ever had in my life.

After what seemed like hours, the doctor escorted Mateo into the room and sat him up next to my head. We were both behind a thin, blue curtain. It was all that separated us from the doctors, who, from the little that I felt, were obviously pulling and tugging away. I'm not sure why this stuck with me, but as the doctor told Mateo he could stand to watch Adrianna enter the world, all I could hear was the *Grease* song "Summer Lovin'" playing on the stereo in the background.

The doctor tried to give me the play by play, and the closer it got to Adrianna's arrival, the less I could hear around me. Once he said her feet were out, I only heard silence. I tuned out the sounds of the doctors behind the screen and the music and just waited to hear her cry. I knew she had made it when Mateo tearfully bent over to tell me, "She's beautiful." I, of course, then lost the grasp of my emotions and tried my best to control the gush of tears. I then heard her—not screaming and crying like the shows on television, but squeaking, just a cute, little, pitiful squeak. At that point, I lost *all* control of emotion. Sound rushed back into the room as tears spilled over my face.

I watched as a doctor rushed her past me to the little table where they checked her over and over again. All I could see was the back of her head and all I could feel was love. I just lay there, crying and crying. I think the doctor was concerned I may be in pain because he continued to ask if I was okay while dabbing my face with gauze. It seemed like an eternity before they finally wrapped her up and handed her to Mateo. I was still unable to hold her, but Mateo placed her cheek close enough for me to kiss it. Her skin was so soft, it felt like I was kissing air. Through my tears, I could barely make out her dark, curly hair and dark blue eyes. All Mateo and I could think to say was, "She's beautiful."

After I was "put back together," I was wheeled to a recovery room where the doctor escorted my mom and dad in to meet Adrianna. I wish I could recall their reactions in detail, but all I could do was look at Adrianna, quietly resting, wrapped up like a burrito in Mateo's arms.

The next two days flew by as visitors came almost hourly to meet my new miracle. I had no doubt that caring for a baby would be hard work, but I never expected to really love and enjoy it, from feeding to changing diapers to almost no sleep. What used to sound like a hard and tiring burden quickly became a blessing of a lifestyle. Changing diapers hourly, learning how to feed, and finding no time for rest were nothing in comparison to the incomprehensible feelings of both love and worry for Adrianna. Every time I held her, I could feel my love for her grow exponentially. It was unexplainable, that feeling of instantly knowing and loving her so deeply because of the nine months I had carried her within me. Giving her up to visitors to be held was much more difficult than I expected. I loved watching others love on her, but couldn't wait to have her back in my own arms.

Leaving the hospital was bittersweet. I was excited to be in the comfort of my own home, but incredibly nervous about no longer having a nurse's aid at the push of a button. My love and worry for her continued to grow after getting home from the hospital. Sometimes it was hard to tell if it was my overwhelming love for her or my hormones that made me cry spontaneously, which I heard was normal for postpartum mothers.

All baby books and guides on sleep schedules and feeding routines had temporarily gone out the window. Before she was born, I considered myself to have it all together and thought I was more than ready for her arrival. After she arrived, my love for her surpassed every other opinion or idea about how to mother a child. When she cried, my heart broke until I found the solution. When she slept, though I knew I should take advantage of that time and sleep myself, I could do nothing but watch her in amazement of God's creation.

The best moments were when, for just a short bit of time, she looked back at me. It was as if she could feel the motherly love I developed for her before she even arrived. I decided to soak in the incredible growing bond between Adrianna and me and figure out the textbook-style parenting later. I was so thankful and glad that God used those nine months to create within me a mother's love for Adrianna. How else would I get through the sleepless nights ahead?

Baby Blues

"I don't know why I'm crying" became a frequent phrase of mine in my first week of motherhood. It was not uncommon for me to burst into tears for no apparent reason. The first night in the hospital, I looked across the room at my little Adrianna, sleeping so innocently in the plastic box-like bed the hospital provided. As I watched her take each small breath and make sweet, sleepy faces, it finally started to sink in that she was here and that I loved her more than life itself. The immense feeling of love and adoration for her sent me right into an unexplainable crying frenzy, which I could only explain by saying, "I just love her so much."

The crying frenzies continued throughout the week and came without warning. My mother was quick to comfort me, without even knowing the cause of my grief. A couple of times in the middle of the night when she was trying to help me soothe Adrianna back to sleep, she was faced with both a crying infant and a crying adult. My mom, along with several other mother-friends of mine, diagnosed these random crying spells as the "Baby Blues." I had read about postpartum depression, but quickly dismissed it since I've never really struggled with negative emotions of that intensity.

One night, as my mom and I finished up Adrianna's bath (which she loved, thank goodness!), I lost it again. That time, however, I recognized that, aside from hormones, I was crying because of exhaustion. Not exhaustion from lack of sleep, but exhaustion from worry. I realized that from the minute Adrianna was born, I had not stopped worrying about her. From one thing to another, I was constantly concerned about her safety and health. When it became too much to bear, I had no way to channel the emotions except to cry it out.

In that moment, it was the fear of her bath that sent me over the edge. I couldn't shake the thoughts of her slipping out of the tub or choking on water. At night, I was concerned about every sound and then every silent moment. I was so fearful she would choke in her sleep or somehow roll over to be face down in her blanket. Adrianna had an abundance of visitors almost daily and with each visitor, my worry only increased. Not because I didn't trust them, but out of my fear and understanding that accidents still happen. These were only a few of the worries that constantly ran through my mind during the first week, and with each intense worry came the tears.

Recognizing that my "baby blues" had a reason behind them was a relief. I was able to think about how to better handle them in the future. After an encouraging talk and prayer with my mom, I was reminded of one of my all-time favorite Bible verses: "Therefore do not worry about tomorrow, for tomorrow will worry about itself. Each day has enough trouble of its own" (Matthew 6:34). This verse, along with many others, made it clear that worrying was a lack of faith. In fact, one might go far enough to say that to worry is to sin. By worrying, I was not trusting that God had complete control of all situations. I was so focused on irrational thoughts that I lost sight of the clear message of God's divine purpose for my daughter in my life.

Although I may always feel some doubt, I could confidently say that I don't believe God would bring me that far for a tragedy to occur. All of the circumstances that had to be in place in order for my daughter to be healthy and safe should be a clear reminder to me that God had Adrianna firmly in His grasp and, as unimaginable as it is, He loves her more than I ever could.

As I zoomed ahead into the days that were passing so quickly, I became prayerful that as I felt the worry start to build and emotions start to rise, that I would be quicker to recognize God's control and slower to let the fears overwhelm me. Rather than being consumed by those "baby blues," I wanted to cry tears of joy for the miracle of life that God was so gracious to bless me with.

Squeaker

"Goooo Yayooooo!" That was what I listened for just before diving off the block at swim meets. My brother and I swam competitively year-round for over 10 years as I grew up, and my parents were there for every race. Swimming consumed our summer days and winter nights. My family practically lived at the pool, as swimming is a sport that sucks up a huge amount of time. We loved it while we did it, though.

Swimming was so relaxing, and though we didn't know it as kids, it was also an awesome form of exercise. Whether I was practicing or just playing, I spent hours splashing around, enjoying the water with friends and family. But when it came to competition, it was a totally different feel. I still get a rush thinking about waiting in line for my turn to race. One of the biggest competitions of the year was called "City County." Swim teams from all over came together at a university pool about an hour from my house. We packed the car full of swim gear, snacks, and games and headed to the meet at the end of every summer.

All the swimmers waited in a huge gymnasium for their events. Once it came time for my event, I had to wait for what seemed like forever in a long line of chairs that led across the gym, down the hallway, and onto the huge pool deck. Once in the pool area, I could look up and see the stands filled with proud parents screaming and cheering on their children. Finding my own parents was nearly impossible, but I always knew they were there. All I had to do was listen for them to yell, "Gooooo Yayooooo!"

Lauren was an incredibly common name and I competed with several other Laurens whose parents would be cheering from the stands. But hearing my parents yell for me was all I needed to get pumped up. I grinned every time I prepared to dive and could hear them in the background. My nickname meant everything to me, not only because it helped me stand out in moments like those, but also because it came from my little brother. If you've ever been around a two-year-old, you know that words don't come easily at first. That's one of my favorite ages for children because it is so darn cute to listen to them speak their gibberish. For my brother, "Lauren" was difficult to say and somehow it turned into "Yayo" (pronounced Yi-Yoh). And Yayo stuck. To this day, my family and some friends use it as my nickname.

The first two weeks of Adrianna's were a blur of sleepless nights and short days, but as we settled in at home, I was able to watch her almost constantly. In just two weeks, I could already see how she had grown and how her unique personality was developing. Before she was born, I wondered if I would be able to pick my own daughter out of a crowd of babies. Two weeks later, I was confident that I could, if not by her distinct physical features, then by her cry. She had her little coos and whimpers as most babies do, but when she was really upset, she gave a cry that was pitiful, heartbreaking, and adorable all at the same time. The only to describe it is to say that each cry was followed by a squeak. When she started squeaking, I knew she was serious about being hungry, wet, or both.

While I don't know what nicknames will develop for her over the years, my brother stuck to calling her "peanut" from the time she was a 10-week-old fetus the size of a peanut. My mom talked about calling her "Little Adri" and my dad created some ridiculous, off-the-wall name that if spelled out would look something like "Cajshagoogoo." At two weeks old, similar to the words of Dory from Finding Nemo, I will call her "Squeaker" and she will be mine. She will be my "Squeaker."

Let Go and Let God

One month after Adrianna's arrival, as I settled into motherhood and I didn't feel so much like a zombie, I started to think about planning for the future again. Before she was born, I filled my time with work, research, and volunteering, all with medical school in mind. Adrianna was still just an idea, an image in my mind. She wasn't really "tangible" yet. I assumed that once she arrived, I would obviously spend a lot of time with her, but that I would also continue to focus on applying to schools and getting ready for the future.

God was quick to correct this mindset. In fact, He started the day I left for the hospital. As I sat with my parents, eating lunch before heading to the doctor, I was in a fog. I had just found out that I had been denied acceptance at my first choice school and, needless to say, I was pretty upset. I couldn't understand why, after working so hard, God would allow me to fail. My parents were quick to encourage me and assure me that it was "meant to be."

All I could think about was how I was sure to get denied everywhere else, and that my future career that could help me support Adrianna was only falling farther away. My mom reminded me that I had much more important things to focus on. She was *so* right!

My mind switched gears as soon as the doctor sent us to the hospital. I wasn't thinking about medical school, but about the long hours leading up to Adrianna's birth. As soon as the moment came, all worries about the future and my career left me. That's not to say that I had given up on my future. I just relinquished all worry and control to the One who has clearly been in control of it all from Day One.

I'm sure it's natural to feel that nothing is more important than your child once they are born, so I don't feel the least bit guilty admitting it. From the moment I met my daughter, I have had no choice but to give all of my love and attention to her and give the rest up to God. I worked hard and did what I needed to do to apply to medical school. From that point forward, I could relax knowing that whatever happened was just as He would have it. For me to become upset about any outcome would be a lack of trust in His ability to do what is best.

As a lifelong "control freak," I plan, organize, and control my surroundings to the best of my ability. Becoming a mother humbled me and forced me to give up control of most things. Though I am still learning how to give up my worry and control over situations with Adrianna, I decided that medical school was a good start. It's amazing how God could use my 3-week-old daughter to teach me a lesson I needed to learn for years. I suppose this was just one glimpse of the many blessings and lessons to come from my sweet baby girl.

Living in the Moment

One day when Adrianna was around one month old, I sat in my living room watching my mom (now called "Gigi") dancing around with Adrianna so I could have a short break. I looked at Adrianna and caught a glimpse of what she would look like in months to come. She seemed so different than she was a month earlier in the hospital. That day was so vivid in my memory; I often wished I could relive it and soak it all in again. Certain moments stood out in my mind, certain images I held onto and wished I had pictures of—the image of my mom, Mateo, and me when the doctor told us we needed to head over to the hospital to have my daughter a week earlier than planned; the image of my dad in the hallway, anxiously pacing back and forth as the nurses prepared me for my C-section; and the image of turning around and looking at my family as I walked down the hall to the operating room. I also distinctly remembered walking into the operating room while thinking to myself, "When I leave this room, she will be here in my arms."

I cherished my first image of Adrianna swaddled up tight in the hospital blanket with a pink and blue hat on as I kissed her cheeks over and over again. I also remembered the image of my mom and dad seeing her for the first time, the image of the first night as I laid awake watching her sleep on my chest, praising God for the best unexpected blessing I could ever have imagined. The list goes on and on.

Those images and memories remained important to me for several reasons. However, the biggest reason is that they are a total affirmation that when I chose life, God changed mine for the better. My pregnancy was certainly full of challenges and hardships, along with excitement and joy, but it all led up to those moments that will forever stand out in my mind as the moments that make up the best day of my life. Unfortunately, moments are exactly that: *moments*. They pass by ever so quickly and all you can do is save the mental snapshots in your mind and hope you never forget them. I wished I could have videotaped every moment from the day Adrianna was born, but I realized how unrealistic that would be.

At one month old, as Adrianna was becoming this alert little person who grew more into herself each day, I couldn't help but wish she would grow more slowly. I tried telling her to slow down, but to no avail. She somehow already grew to be a month old and almost two pounds heavier. I was sure she wished I would accept her inevitable growth, because she very clearly did not enjoy it when I tried to squeeze on the onesies she wore at the hospital. I could easily see myself becoming a hoarder one day, since each article of clothing retained a special memory of her in my heart.

Whereas a few months earlier I was praying time would pass more quickly, instead I found myself praying the time would slow down to a snail's pace. I loved each and every day I could spend with Adrianna and thanked God every night that I had the flexibility to spend two whole months with her before heading back to work. But that time was half over, and I became tearful thinking about being away from her for an extended period of time.

Moment by moment I am watching as the miracle of life continues outside of my womb. I am much less anxious now and have lost the "baby blues", praise God! I still get anxious from time to time and there are many more milestones to come, I am sure. Although a lot of my time is spent changing diapers, feeding Adrianna and catching up on sleep here and there, I am trying to cherish every moment that passes by. Call me crazy, but Adrianna already seems so big to me. I don't think God calls us to live in the moment from the standpoint that we blindly face the future and ignore consequences of our actions. But I do think that for now, as this precious time is ticking away, He would want me to live in each moment with my daughter, soaking in every cuddle, kiss and coo. I'm sure I will love every stage of her life as much as the next, but if I could hold her here for awhile, I would. And I would love every dirty diaper, every sleepless night... every blessed moment.

Simple Pleasures

Not a moment went by with Adrianna that I didn't wish I knew what she was thinking, especially when she was crying despite having a full tummy, plenty of rest, and a clean diaper. But if I had to choose just one moment to read her mind, it would be when she was looking at her "dots." My aunt sent a large package full of fun baby books to read to Adrianna, one of which was the "Art for Baby" book. The book is comprised of very plain black and white images that are easy for infants to focus on, like a big flower, a face, or a carrot. But we quickly realized that Adrianna was particularly interested in the page covered with a bunch of polka dots. By eight weeks, she began to show a little smile here and there and even let out, what seems to be, the beginnings of a laugh when provoked by her Pappy. A few silly noises and faces could bring out her smiles, but they were still very rare. That was, until I revisited the dots with her. As soon as I turned to the page with the dots, she used her whole face to grin and let out an adorable baby "ooooh," which I assumed would soon transform into a laugh. I was, perhaps, more tickled than she was as I marveled at how beautiful her smile was.

As I started trying to envision what her laugh would sound like in the months to come, it hit me how silly it was that she was laughing at those simple little dots. In that moment, for Adrianna, those dots were the most amazing thing in the world. For a mom, of course, it is wonderful how easily entertained young children can be. But polka dots? It doesn't get much simpler than that. It made me envy her a little. At age 22, it took a lot more to keep me entertained because I've become so desensitized to the simple pleasures of life. I very often overlook some of the finer details that I'm sure God created for us to enjoy.

I was delighted that my daughter was already finding things to admire and enjoy. Through her little smiles and laughs, I could see a beautiful personality developing. I hadn't been as diligent as I had hoped at keeping track of all her baby milestones, nor was I able to write down the little quirks I loved about her in that stage, which were certain to fade out of my memory over time. Although I hoped to write these down in her journal and on her milestone calendar, I did manage to type out a list to share here. This one's for you Adrianna Grace!

- The first night in the hospital, I stayed up all night watching you snore. Not a manly snore by any means, but an adorable little squeak. In fact, I have a video of it so I'm hoping to still have it one day to share with you.
- I think you have bad dreams sometimes, because when you are sleeping, you will make the most pitiful, pouty face, and whimper a little.
- You sneeze whenever the sun shines on your face and generally your sneezes come in two's. Sometimes you even startle yourself.
- Your Pappy was the first one to make you consciously smile and laugh. Of all noises, he chose to stick his tongue out at you and make that

"Thbbbbpt" sound. You LOVED it! He also calls you "Kajagoogoo" and "boo boo" and you focus really hard on him when he talks to you.

- If it weren't for those crazy hands of yours, eating and sleeping may be easier. Your hands are constantly moving and constantly up at your face, just like in all of your ultrasound pictures. A lot of times, it looks like you are reaching for something.
- No matter where we are, inside or outside, you instantly want to look straight up, even if there is nothing there. I like to imagine you can see Jesus. Whatever it is you see, it must be pretty fantastic because you look at it a lot.
- You stick your tongue out ALL the time! When you are in your car seat, which you HATE, the shoulder pads squish your cheeks together and your tongue sticks out. You look annoyed but it's so cute!
- Those crazy hiccups! You get them all the time, usually right when I have put you to sleep.
- You work extra hard to fill that diaper of yours. Let's just say you make it known when I'm about to have to change your diaper.
- You love dots! Anything with dots on it, especially black and white dots. As I write this, Pappy is playing with you on your baby jungle gym which is adorned with black and white dots and you are amazed!
- Your eye color is still keeping us guessing. Sometimes they look brown, sometimes they look green. I can't wait to see which color stays!
- When you get excited or tickled about something, you start kicking like crazy and blowing little bubbles! I am anxious for you to be big enough to fit in one

- of those doorway jumper toys. You are going to be a fantastic jumper!
- As if crying wasn't pitiful enough, you squeak too! You've turned me into a crazy mom who can't stand to hear you cry for longer than a minute.
- You slept in your crib for the first time last night, September 5th, 2011. Gigi put you to sleep in there, so of course when you woke up at 3am and I fed you, you wouldn't go back in there for anything. Somehow you ended up in bed cuddling with me, so I won't complain.
- You LOVE music, especially piano music. Gigi plays for you sometimes and you just watch her in amazement. Since I have no musical talent, I play songs for you on my iPod and we dance around while I sing terribly. It helps distract you when I change your diaper, too. I'm already praying you didn't get my music genes (or lack thereof).
- Sometimes you look at me with one eyebrow raised, as if you're saying, "What the heck?" It's adorable.
- If you are just slightly tired, but don't want to sleep, you literally fall asleep with one eye open. It's as if you're daring me to put you down . . . so I don't.
- You have talons! Not really, but your nails are dangerous. No matter how often I cut them, you still manage to scratch me.
- Most importantly, you are loved . . . *SO* loved! There are already so many people who love you, including me. Don't you ever forget it!

For me, Adrianna, you are my "dots," my simple pleasure, in every single way.

The Terrible, Awful, Good-for-Nothing Car Seat

After having Adrianna, every time I saw a pregnant woman, I wanted to tell her that the little sleep she was getting was actually an amazing amount of sleep and to enjoy every moment of it. That's not to say I disliked my middle-of-the-night wake-up times, by any means. I loved the sweet cuddle time that came out of those late night feedings very much, and I'm sure I will one day wish they had continued for longer. When I was pregnant, I thought that waking up around 4am every night for all of five minutes due to a sudden kick or wiggle from Adrianna was causing me to feel sleep deprived. I obviously did not know what sleep deprived really was.

Aside from sleep, I also reminisced about the exciting times I spent at Toys R' Us planning and preparing for Adrianna. I tried so hard to imagine what each outfit would look like on her or what it would be like to use all the baby accessories. Even after several weeks, it was still a little surreal to see her in the nursery wearing some of those outfits. She was, of course, way cuter than I imagined.

The thing I was most excited to purchase, however, turned out to cause the most problems. I spent hours and hours researching the latest, greatest brands to find the absolute safest one based on customer reviews. After finally deciding on one, I saved up my money from work, along with several gift cards, and made a special trip to Toys R' Us to buy what I now call, "the terrible, awful, good-for-nothing car seat!"

I was so excited when my dad and I first put it in my car, which was several weeks before Adrianna was born. I spent a lot of time driving each day because my house was about 15 minutes from town and 25 minutes from where I worked as a volunteer researcher. I spent a lot of that time imagining my little girl sitting in the back, smiling, looking around, or drifting off to sleep.

Her first ride in the car seat was a piece of cake by comparison, because we were leaving the hospital and she was still averaging 20 hours of sleep every day, so she slept the whole way home and I cried the whole way home. I soon discovered during the car rides to follow that the safest, latest, greatest car seat was actually incredibly uncomfortable for her. The seat came with a removable infant insert that could only be removed once Adrianna was eleven pounds, and so far she was only about nine. The insert was there to provide cushion, but instead, it forced her shoulders up into her cheeks and her knees up into her stomach. Each car ride caused me a significant amount of anxiety. Unless I could time it perfectly so she would be asleep before I placed her in the seat, the ride consisted of a crying fit that ended with both of us in tears. In fact, the seven-minute ride home from my mom's church took 30 minutes one day because I pulled over three times just to console her. As mentioned before, her cry was pitiful! I couldn't stand to let her cry it out.

I finally regained a bit of common sense and realized the infant insert could be adjusted so that the cushions would fit higher up on her head and give her more space. After I made the change, she wasn't so frustrated sitting in it and became a little more comfortable driving her around. All it took was a two-minute adjustment . . . but, such is life.

I often got so consumed by a problem that I completely overlooked the easy, obvious solutions. If I had just taken more time to think of possible solutions rather than get all wrapped up in the anxiety of the next car trip, I may have saved myself some worry and certainly some tears.

I was sure there would be many more tantrums in the car, so I could only pray that with each one, I would be able to quickly remind myself that Adrianna wouldn't remember them one day. In the moment, all I could think of was how she was back there crying out for her mother who was ignoring her. Regardless of the tantrums, I'm sure one day, when it's no longer needed, it will be hard to get rid of that terrible, awful, good-for-nothing car seat.

Bump in the Road

I had to plan an extra 10 minutes or more into my daily agenda because of the massive construction sites along the street leading to my house. Every day, I expected to see the poor construction guy standing by the side of the road holding up the reversible "Slow" or "Stop" sign. I felt so bad for him, having to wear jeans, a long-sleeve shirt, a construction vest, and a hard hat in the summer heat.

While waiting in the long line of frustrated people, I wondered how many times he accidentally lost track of which side of the sign he was showing. I pictured the unsuspecting car impatiently whipping by, having complete trust in the man with the sign, only to drive head first into oncoming traffic. Needless to say, after playing out this scenario in my mind enough times, I took the "Slow" side of the sign very seriously—not only so that I don't find myself mindlessly driving into the front seat of a Mack truck, but also because of the three consecutive annoying bumps in the road as a result of the construction.

Adrianna didn't hate her car seat as much anymore. Either that, or I'd been lucky enough to time each trip so that she had a full tummy and a dry diaper. Regardless of her state of mind, each one of those bumps evoked fear in me. I saw them coming and eased onto the brakes, hoping and praying that they wouldn't shake the car so violently if I was going 40 instead of 45. I'm didn't even know why I worried about it so much. Those bumps never proved to be the reason for a tantrum. If anything, they merely startled her and she soon forgot it ever happened. Yet, I still found myself holding my breath at each bump.

One night as I drove home with Adrianna asleep in her car seat, I got to those darn bumps and, like always, slowed down and prepared for the worst. And, like always, nothing happened. In fact, I think she was sleeping so soundly that she didn't even feel it. It made me think about how I react to my "bumps in the road." I don't think I can go a week without having some sort of bump to get over. Praise God, more recently my bumps have consisted of dealing with baby problems, like cleaning up a blowout diaper in public.

Just like when I'm driving, I let those bumps slow me down and I hesitated to face them. Most of the time, I took a good long look at the bump before trying to get over it, which I eventually realized was totally the wrong mindset. If I've learned anything from this whole experience, it's that God is in control. So why was I letting such comparatively small things slow me down in daily life? Instead of thinking, "Oh geez, how should I handle this?" I should be thinking, "Oh Jesus, how should I handle this?" If I could be quicker to look to Him for guidance, I would be less hesitant with the bumps of my life. In fact, I would probably be more inclined to approach them with confidence and reassurance that they won't slow me down in the greater scheme of things.

As for the literal bumps in my road, I don't think speeding over them confidently would end very well.

Even though she was only two months old, she was already picking up on my emotions. For my daughter to be able to sense my anxiety over something as small as a bump in the road was definitely not the outcome I wanted. After all, she'll have her own bumps to face one day.

Baby Talk

"Love the Lord your God with all your heart and with all your soul and with all your strength. These commandments that I give you today are to be on your hearts. <u>Impress them on your children</u>. Talk about them when you sit at home and when you walk along the road, when you lie down and when you get up." — Deuteronomy 6:5-7, emphasis mine

At 12 weeks, Adrianna was obviously not talking yet, but she surely did try. When she was in the right mood, I could get a small "goo" or gurgle in response to some short phrases or sounds. She smiled with each one. This could go on for 10 or 15 minutes sometimes before she got tired or bored and moved on to the next thought. Those short few minutes were so precious to me. They gave me a glimpse of our mother-daughter talks that I hoped would continue to be frequent in the future. I often looked to my relationship with my own mother when thinking about how I hoped my relationship with Adrianna would be. Although I don't really remember what my mom and I talked about when I was little, I know each conversation built upon the one before it, eventually creating an indescribably close relationship; an unbreakable bond. I have an incredible desire to create a similar relationship with Adrianna, if not the same.

The above verse in Deuteronomy is such a clear command to moms for us to be in constant conversation with our children, and for that conversation to be significant! What could be more important than teaching my daughter about her Creator? The One who knew her and loved her before I even could. I tried to incorporate Him more into our conversations. For example, I tried to start her morning routine with some (admittedly bad) singing of "This is the day that the Lord has made." When I remembered during the day, I tried to insert comments about His creation or say quick prayers to end tantrums. My prayer was that eventually she would consider God to be a normal, important part of conversation and that she would have confidence in speaking about Him. Even though at this age she may only giggle at the things I say and respond with "ah-goo," our baby talk will one day turn to toddler talk, and then child talk, and on to teen talk, and adult talk. My hope has always been that she would love the Lord her God with all her heart and with all her soul and with all her strength.

On Wings Like Eagles

In the weeks after Adrianna's birth, I struggled to shake thoughts of the previous year and how quickly the time has passed since I found out I was pregnant. Of one thing I was sure: I could not be where I was without God. All of the prayer and Christian guidance and support gave me the strength I needed to make it to this point in the journey.

When Adrianna was 12 weeks old, I was blessed with the opportunity to share my story with nearly 500 people at a fundraising banquet for the Blue Ridge Women's Center. Thanks to some serious stage fright, I've never been much of a public speaker, so I anticipated being incredibly nervous. But seeing all of those people there had the reverse effect and actually made me feel encouraged and loved. To see such a large group of people, including some of my dear friends from church, willing to support a cause that so powerfully impacted my life, gave me so much joy. When I spoke, I wanted them to hear, more than anything, that their prayers and support would go farther than they may ever know. For me, it meant a new start, a new life, and a new future.

After sharing my story and talking about my unplanned miracle, my mom brought Adrianna up on stage so that I could introduce her. As people stood to applaud, all I could think about was how Adrianna and our story together made the past year worth every tear, every struggle, and every worry. I am already so proud of the little person that she is because I have been blessed to see all of the pieces of her life so far fit perfectly together from the beginning. I knew God had even bigger plans and purposes for her life in the future. I couldn't wait to see it unfold, day by day. Just as the days flew by like seconds, I was sure the years would soon seem like minutes.

As November 29th drew closer, I couldn't help but be thankful for all that had happened since that same day the previous year, when I found out I was pregnant. In addition to my family, friends, and close acquaintances who were all praying for me, I also found strength and encouragement from how many of them read my blog. In less than a year, I was been blessed to share my blog almost 8,000 times with people in over 20 different countries. Whether I ever know the ways or not, I prayed that God would use my story somehow. Knowing that my story could possibly help just one other person was worth it.

As time continued to fly forward, I could be confident that the same God who brought me this far would continue to carry me into the future on wings like eagles, while providing me with everything I need to get through the obstacles I face.

"Do you not know? Have you not heard? The Lord is the everlasting God, the Creator of the ends of the earth. He will not grow tired or weary, and His understanding no one can fathom. He gives strength to the weary and increases the power of the weak. Even youths grow tired and weary, and young men stumble and fall; but those who hope in the Lord will renew their strength. They will

soar <u>on wings like eagles;</u> they will run and not grow weary, they will walk and not be faint." – Isaiah 40:28-31, emphasis mine

A Different "Forever" Kind of Love

There is a hidden-treasure of a resort called "The Homestead" not too far from my home. When I was a little girl, my family went to the resort for their ski slopes, hot springs, and beautiful scenery. It is an old resort that has been restored to have a high class feel to it. Every night they held a fancy dinner in their exquisite dining room. We got all dressed up and enjoyed the classy, live music as they served a five-star meal.

My fondest memory of the Homestead is of my brother and me dancing on the dance floor as people "awww'd" at us. At the time, I think he was embarrassed, but it made me feel like a princess. In one part of the Homestead, there was a big double staircase that led down to a room with huge windows overlooking the gardens. To the right, large double doors led into a gorgeous ballroom with big, sparkling chandeliers. Being young and imaginative, I loved to daydream about one day having my wedding there. I could see myself slowly drifting down one side of the staircase and my father on the other. We would meet in the middle and walk down the second set of stairs together, then on to my Prince Charming waiting for me at the altar in front of the big window. Afterward, the reception would take place in the ballroom and close friends and family could stay the night in the resort. This dream stuck with me for years, and even before finding out I was pregnant, I still had the same vision for myself, just as I had so many other intentions.

An obvious aspect of my pregnancy that I didn't touch on in this book was the whole "before marriage" part. It was obviously implied and for a long time I didn't feel it was a necessary part to share. Honestly, it's part of my story that still upsets me from time to time. For years I had clung to a big dream of a wedding day, and for a while, it seemed as if I had ruined that dream completely. After Adrianna was born, I was right at the age when a lot of my friends and acquaintances were getting engaged and married. To see others living out a dream I had so anxiously awaited was undoubtedly difficult.

But a friend reminded me, "Just because your plans aren't happening right now, doesn't mean God is saying they never will." Instead of first having that incredible love story that leads to a dream wedding and then a beautiful family, God had given me a different "forever" kind of love. Adrianna became my whole world, my one and only, and my everything for the time being. I sometimes wondered how I could even have enough love left over to share with anyone else.

Although it wasn't the love story I expected to come first, it is exactly that: a love story. First and foremost came God's love for me; none of this would have been possible without Him. His love and grace sent me flying through a whirlwind nine months of varied emotions, all of which somehow molded into one, great big, undeniable love, along with the obvious miracle of life.

God gave me the opportunity to experience a love greater than any other. Although my sweet daughter came before the white dress and the flowers and the long-awaited walk down the aisle, God gave me comfort and joy in the love I found in her. My future wedding was in His hands. I would be lying if I said I didn't still dream about my wedding day from time to time. However, my dreams included a much more specific idea for a flower girl.

Just Keep Swimming, Swimming, Swimming

To have Adrianna in a pool with me for the first time was an indescribable joy. I spent 12 years of my life swimming competitively, then spent a lot of time putting that skill to work by teaching swimming lessons for children at the local YMCA. I loved teaching lessons, mainly because of how much fun I had working with the kids. They kept me entertained with their cute antics, and I have endless stories about funny things they said. One came to mind after swimming with Adrianna.

During one of my swim lessons, I had a 4-year-old boy who required a lot of bribing just to get him in the water. I had all kinds of different games and things to say to try and comfort the kids who were fearful, such as putting on the "magic backpack" (those square Styrofoam floaties you strap to your back). But this little boy had his own self-soothing tactic. As soon as I pulled him from the wall, he began singing that song from "Finding Nemo": "just keep swimming, just keep swimming, swimming, swimming." I tried very hard to keep myself from laughing! But I loved that he had found a way to make the challenge easier for himself.

I was anxious to share my love for swimming with my daughter. In fact, I bought her little polka-dotted swimsuit several months before she was born. Back then, I had such different images in my head about what she would look like in it, where she would wear it first, etc. But our first trip to the pool blew my ideas out of the water. She was much more adorable than I dreamed, and her first swimming lesson was much more fun than I had envisioned. She loved the water and was so entranced by the light reflecting off of it. We bounced her around, splashed a little, and even practiced a tiny bit of actual swim skills, like kicking—skills she would soon learn when she had more control of her body. At the end of our time there, we decided to get brave and for a brief moment put her face in the water. She was very unsure about it at first and whined a little, but she quickly realized she was fine and enjoyed doing it a second and third time.

To see her comfortable in the water was so encouraging to me. The years I spent teaching swim lessons were full of many children who had an indescribable fear of the water and would have done anything to avoid getting their faces wet. My hope was that regardless of whether or not she chose to swim as a sport in the future, she would be comfortable in the water and be able to swim safely.

Being open to trying new things was a lesson I learned many times from my parents. They understood the importance of having an open mind. Thanks to that open mindset mentality, I participated in every sport possible throughout my school career. I'm sure they may have kicked themselves a little after realizing that before I could drive myself places, they would be escorting me around town to each of my events. But I know they enjoyed seeing me have fun and do well at some of the sports I chose.

I couldn't wait to see what Adrianna would choose to do or what passions she would have in life. Whether it was swimming or not, I hoped she would also appreciate trying new things and possess a perseverance for the things she finds challenging. I prayed I would show her how to take each new challenge to her heavenly Father and rely on Him for the same strength He gave me when I have needed it.

One Year Ago Today

One year ago today, I never would have guessed the innumerable blessings that would come from the positive pregnancy test I held in my hand. I was sure of the facts: "I'm pregnant. I'm going to have a baby in nine months. My family and friends are going to be shocked." But I had no idea what amazing things God could or would do in those short nine months, and now, 365 days. Then, that test represented a whirlwind of fear, anger, anxiety, worry, shame, and more. Now, that test represents incredible blessings I never could have imagined, the most obvious being my beautiful daughter. But along with her came other blessings, like spiritual growth, a greater appreciation for family and friends, and the courage to share my story with the hope of helping others. Back then, I never imagined how thankful I would become for those test results. Honestly, it couldn't be more perfect timing than at the end of the season of Thanksgiving and the beginning of the season of Christmas, the greatest unplanned pregnancy of all!

I can't believe how fast it all flew by and I can only hope the time slows down from here. My little peanut was only the size of a sesame seed a year ago. Now she is a whopping 14 pounds and 24 inches. At only four months old, she has developed such a sweet and fun personality. I enjoy every minute of our time together. Although smiles, giggles, and cuddles may be very unexciting to some people, for me each one is just as exciting as the first time. I am so proud of her milestones, so in celebration of one year together, I'll list the following for her future reading pleasure:

- Along with Peanut, Boo-Boo, Kajagoogoo, and Squeaker, you are also now called Booger, Baby Girl, and sometimes even your real name, Adrianna.

- You laugh—*a lot*! Especially when anyone shakes their head from side to side and makes any kind of silly noise, like "sssssss" or "thbbbbpt."

- We found where you are ticklish, but I'll keep it a secret for a while to save you from the Tickle Monster.

- The Velcro swaddle is no longer a match for your Houdini-like moves. I wake up every morning to you smiling with both arms above your head out of the swaddle. I would eliminate the swaddle altogether, but you haven't quite perfected putting yourself to sleep yet.

- Speaking of sleep, you are great at it! Anywhere between eight to ten hours a night! Thank you, thank you, thank you! You also practically slept the whole way to the beach and back last week! Bravo!

- You met your entire family at the beach last week, and they adore you! So much, in fact, I rarely held you. There was always someone wanting to steal some of your cuddles.

- While at the beach, we spent lots of time swimming in the pool. You have almost mastered raising your arms and dropping them to cause a splash. You think it's great!

- Just as I expected, you are fantastic at the Johnny Jump Up! I've known since I was 20 weeks pregnant that you would be an active little booger. In fact, I think every nurse and doctor I saw said that as soon as you were able to move yourself, I would be in trouble!

- You try to sing along when there is someone else singing. You first did this with Gigi while she played the piano (and yes, we have it on video). You've done it a few times in the car with me. It kind of sounds like screaming right now, but I *love* it!

- Speaking of screaming, you do that a lot, too. Not like singing, more like talking, especially when you know you aren't getting attention. It's as if you are reminding us that you are there. You also just do it because you like to hear the different sounds you can make. It's adorable.

- You love your hands. You chew on them all day, every day. They are your favorite toy.

- You got your four-month shots yesterday and you only cried for two minutes. Then you started laughing and talking and you've been happy ever since!

- You talk to Pappy a lot, but I think it's because he actually talks back with the sounds you use, so you probably think he's just a much bigger baby.

- You can hold your head up really well and you can almost sit up. You like to stand up when we hold you, but it makes me feel like you are growing up too fast, so then I make you lay back down.

- Your little tummy can't handle the cheaper, more common formulas like most babies. Nope, you demand Nutramigen, the most expensive formula that smells quite awful, but whatever makes you happy!

- Last, but not least, I love you forever and always. From as small as a sesame seed to wherever you end up, I couldn't be more thankful for you, my sweet miracle.

This is My Story, This is My Song

We finally decided on a Sunday that would work for Adrianna to be "dedicated"—my church's version of "christening." It had to be a Sunday when my mom wasn't working, so we made the quick, almost mindless decision to have it at the five o'clock service on Christmas day. Once the decision was made, there was not much more thought put into it.

This whole journey with Adrianna started with my "impossible" happening. I clung to the story of Mary and the verse from Luke 1:37, "For nothing is impossible with God," as I faced my similar, yet completely different unplanned pregnancy. Mary was obviously carrying the Son of God. AWESOME! Which may or may not have made her initial reaction a bit calmer. But I know her interaction with the angel Gabriel had to have made things seem a little less impossible for her, just as my interaction with the Blue Ridge Women's Center, my close friends, and family did.

As my pregnancy progressed, Mary's story continued to play a significant role of encouragement and healing as my family knelt to pray for me in Israel at the place where Gabriel approached Mary, a moment I couldn't wait to tell Adrianna about. Mary's story continued to be a stronghold for me as I faced unexpected challenges in my pregnancy and then even after Adrianna was born. As God called me to share my story to hundreds of people, in my fear I looked to that verse for strength and encouragement.

Then my mother made the connection that Christmas day was the most perfect day for Adrianna to be dedicated. What better day than the day Mary was able to look at her newborn and see how God had made her challenging and seemingly impossible situation possible. I loved that Adrianna would be dedicated to her heavenly Father the same day that He dedicated His son to saving us all. And as I was sure Mary did, I would feel inexplicably proud of that dedication.

Throughout my journey, I have enjoyed the ways God has shown me my simple little relations to Mary and her story. Many mornings as I drove to work, I sang loudly along with a CD, "This is my story, this is my song. Praising my savior, all the day long. Perfect submission, all is at rest. I in my Savior am happy and blessed. Watching and waiting, looking above, filled with His goodness, lost in His love."

Although that song was not in existence at the time Jesus was born, I am sure Mary must have felt the same way I do when I relate to the words. Although unexpected, this is my story. This is my life song. I praise my Savior all the day long for the wonderful works He has done in me through my experience. I submitted to His will, which seemed so terrifyingly impossible, and He ultimately brought me to a place of peace and rest. Now in Him I am so happy and blessed by my sweet, unexpected miracle, Adrianna! I still watch and wait for

Him, looking to Him always for guidance. I am filled with His goodness and lost in His amazingly abundant, unconditional love that overflows daily to my daughter.

On Christmas Day, a most special day, I gave up my daughter to Him so that one day, amidst the trials of her own, she, too, will be able to confidently sing: "This is my story, this is my song."

About the Author

Lauren lives in Winston-Salem. NC with her husband and three children. She completed her Masters degree and works as a full time Physician Assistant. When she's not attending basketball games, soccer games and swimming lessons, she enjoys volunteering her free time to a local pregnancy center providing ultrasounds and support to other women who find themselves facing an unexpected blessing. Please visit LaurenUrrea.wordpress.com for more information about Lauren and booking for your next event.

Made in the USA
Columbia, SC
15 March 2019